82624

INDIA

I

GREAT

INDIAN LIFE
IN THE
UPPER
GREAT LAKES

11,000 B.C. to A.D. 1800

By George Irving Quimby

THE UNIVERSITY OF CHICAGO PRESS

A CONTRIBUTION OF CHICAGO NATURAL HISTORY MUSEUM

Library of Congress Catalog Number: 60-11799

The University of Chicago Press, Chicago & London
The University of Toronto Press, Toronto 5, Canada

© 1960 by The University of Chicago
Published 1960. Second Impression 1961
Composed by the University of Chicago Press
and printed by Photopress, Inc.
Chicago, Illinois, U.S.A.

For **HELEN**

SEDNA

EDWARD

JOHN

and **ROBERT**

This book, in part at least, is the product of a lifelong interest in the Indians of the Upper Great Lakes region. As a young boy in western Michigan some forty years ago I remember looking for stone arrowheads in the hollows among the sand dunes. I also remember Ottawa women in summertime selling baskets woven of sweet grass.

In 1930 I collected my first ethnological specimen, a birchbark bucket, from a maple grove near an Indian settlement on Garden Island in northern Lake Michigan. As an undergraduate and graduate student majoring in anthropology at the University of Michigan I concentrated on problems concerning the Upper Great Lakes Indians. And although I have since worked in other regions and with different kinds of anthropological problems, I have always retained an interest in the Lakes area.

I began this book in 1956 and completed the writing of it in the spring of 1959. But not all of my time was spent in writing. Most time, in fact, was spent in organizing the data, studying museum and private collections of artifacts, visiting archeological sites, making archeological surveys of areas where data were lacking, relating sites to former beach levels, and reading site reports and other background material.

The book was written topic by topic and period by period, and as gaps appeared in the knowledge I made study trips or read various reports in an attempt to fill these gaps. Thus, in effect, each chapter was treated as an independent project in terms of both research and writing.

The substance of this book has been used several times in my courses at the University of Chicago. Some of the chapters or parts of them have appeared in the *Chicago Natural History Museum Bulletin* during 1957–59, and part of one chapter has been printed in *American Antiquity*. But two-thirds of this book have not previously been published and this is the first time that all of the chapters have appeared in the context that I intended for them.

This book was not written for the specialist, although I hope that some of the data and ideas will be of use to him. It is aimed more toward the interested lay reader and the introductory student or someone who has a general regional interest in the Upper Great Lakes.

My orientation and points of view have been influenced beneficially by Douglas S. Byers, Emerson F. Greenman, James B. Griffin, Will C. McKern, Robert Ritzenthaler, George M. Stanley, and Albert C. Spaulding. I am grateful to the many museums and individuals who allowed me to see their collections and provided me with information. I am particularly grateful to Chicago Natural History Museum (formerly Field Museum of Natural History) for providing the time and money that made this book possible.

The illustrations have been provided by the staff of Chicago Natural History Museum. Some of the maps and all of the drawings are the work of Gustaf Dalstrom. Many of the photographs were made by John Bayalis and Homer V. Holdren.

CONTENTS

LIST OF ILLUSTRATIONS

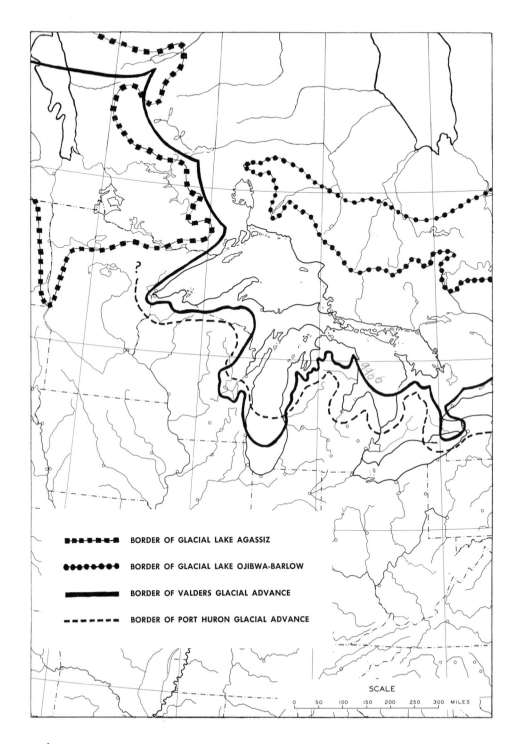

BORDER OF GLACIAL LAKE AGASSIZ

BORDER OF GLACIAL LAKE OJIBWA-BARLOW

BORDER OF VALDERS GLACIAL ADVANCE

BORDER OF PORT HURON GLACIAL ADVANCE

SCALE

0   50   100   150   200   250   300   MILES

xiv

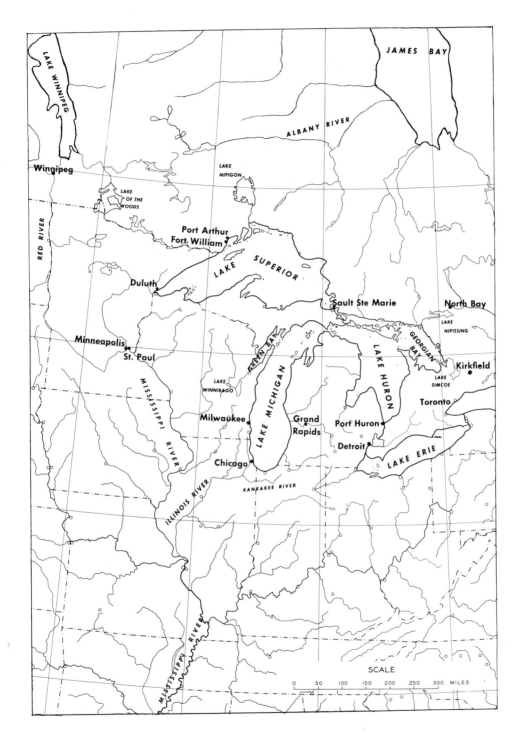

1. AN INTRODUCTION
TO THE UPPER GREAT LAKES
REGION

The Upper Great Lakes region embraces more than 200,000 square miles, comprising the drainage basins of Lake Superior, Lake Huron, and Lake Michigan. It includes almost all of Michigan, much of Ontario, a considerable part of Wisconsin, small portions of Minnesota and Indiana, and a small part of Illinois adjacent to Chicago.

The history of the region is rather well known, but it covers only the last few centuries. Much less is known of the prehistory, which goes back to the latter part of the ice age some 13,000 years ago.

The history of the region, based upon documentary researches of historians, is concerned primarily with the story of white explorers, missionaries, traders, and settlers. The prehistory of the region is the story of the Indian and his changing environment during the thousands of years from 11,000 B.C. to A.D. 1600.

The story of the Indian and his environment is based upon the researches of archeologists, glacial geologists, and specialists in natural history. Because there are no written documents, the data of prehistory must be gathered from the unintentional records left by the Indians—fragments of tools, weapons, utensils, and ornaments found in refuse heaps or in the dirt of old dwelling floors, or in old hearths or pits; the objects placed in graves; weapon points lost in hunting; and articles lost or discarded around former camps or villages.

The data used to reconstruct the prehistoric environments come from bones of fossil animals; the land forms and deposits recognized and interpreted by glacial geologists; and the remains of fossil plants and trees studied by specialist botanists. From all of these and other sources of information, made available by scientists in various fields, it is possible to reconstruct the histories and habitats of people who left no written records.

Until about 7000 B.C. a continental glacier was the principal element in the geography of the Upper Great Lakes region. After that time water became the dominant factor, as it is today.

The Upper Great Lakes region is a product of the Ice Age. The drainage patterns, land forms, and soils are all results of glaciation. The advancing glaciers of the Ice Age covered all of the Upper Great Lakes region, grinding down rock masses, gouging out basins, and pulverizing stone into sand and soil. Great masses of glacial ice, hundreds, if not thousands, of feet thick, depressed the land and drove all living things from the region.

At the peak of glaciation the Upper Great Lakes region was devoid of all life —an icy waste. With the retreat of the glaciers, living things entered the region. First came the plant life, then came the animal life, and finally came human life—American Indians.

At present Lake Superior has about 31,800 square miles of water surface; Lake Huron, about 23,000 square miles; and Lake Michigan, 22,400 square miles. At various times during the past 13,000 years these areas of water have been much larger than now and at some periods much smaller.

There were at times other great lakes. Lake Agassiz was a tremendous body of water as large as lakes Superior, Huron, and Michigan combined. During much of its existence it drained eastward to the Superior basin. Another large lake now vanished was Lake Ojibwa-Barlow, lying north of Huron and Superior basins. These additional lakes, before their disappearance, more than doubled the water surface of the present Upper Great Lakes region.

The ice, present prior to 7000 B.C. and lasting north of the Superior basin until about 4500 B.C., precluded the establishment of plants and animals as well as people.

Water surface, the other geographical factor, particularly significant after 7000 B.C., was either an obstacle or a tremendous advantage, depending upon the cultural adjustment to it by the Indians. To a people without boats of some kind, large lakes and rivers are natural barriers. The possession of suitable boats renders the large lakes and rivers as well as the small ones the avenues of transportation and settlement.

When the white men first encountered the Indians of the Upper Great Lakes region the numerous waterways were the highways. In their birchbark canoes the Indians traveled along the coasts of the great lakes and all the streams and rivers of the interior parts of the region. All villages and camps were on streams, rivers, or lakes. Although the use of the canoe was limited to the non-winter months, it was the primary means of travel and transport over most of the year. And although other cultural or environmental forces may have operated, waterways as means of travel, transport, and settlement were the most important single geographic factor of the region after 7000 B.C.

The Indians of the Upper Great Lakes almost certainly had boats of some kind as early as 7000 B.C. We know this because some occupation sites of that period have been found in areas that at the time would have been islands only suitable for summer living. Moreover, settlement patterns of the region from around 7000 B.C. to A.D. 1800 clearly demonstrate the dependence of the Indians upon the lakes, streams, and rivers.

In view of such a dependence upon waterways in historic as well as prehistoric times, it seems most fitting to define the Upper Great Lakes region in terms of area of drainage basin.

The natural drainage basin of present-day Lake Superior embraces about 81,000 square miles, that of Lake Huron about 72,600 square miles, and that of Lake Michigan about 68,000 square miles.

As now constituted, the total area, defined by drainage, includes about 222,-000 square miles of land and water surface. In the periods when the extinct Lake Agassiz and Lake Ojibwa-Barlow were part of the Upper Great Lakes region, the area defined by drainage would have been double or perhaps triple that extent.

The present-day Upper Great Lakes region had a forest cover of southeastern hardwoods (oak-hickory) in the extreme southern portion, a northeastern hardwood forest (birch-beech-maple-hemlock) in the middle portions, and a northeastern pine forest (white, Norway, and jack pine) in the northern portions. Although there are some sizable areas of spruce-fir in the Upper Great Lakes region, the main northern coniferous forest (spruce-fir) now lies north of the area.

Today the climate of the region varies with latitude. Most of the area possesses a continental forest climate with harsh winters, but the southern portion has a moderate marine forest climate with mild winters and a small part of the northern periphery of the region has a continental taiga climate with very severe winters.

The Upper Great Lakes region had a rich fauna at the time of its discovery by Europeans. There were many different species of mammals, birds, and fishes of economic importance to the Indians. Of large game animals, only bear and deer were found throughout the region, but bison and elk were present in the southern portions of the area and moose and caribou lived in the northern parts.

Of the smaller mammals the marten, fisher, wolverine, and lynx were found in the northern part of the region and the opossum, mountain lion, and bob-cat occurred in the southern portion. The raccoon, weasel, mink, otter, fox, coyote, wolf, woodchuck, squirrel, rabbit, beaver, muskrat, and skunk were found throughout the region. The porcupine was absent in the extreme south and the badger was absent in the extreme north.

It has been estimated that a band of 50 Indians, 28 adults and 22 children, could subsist five days on the flesh of 1 moose; four days on the flesh of 1 elk; two days on 1 bear, one day on 2 deer, and one day on 40 rabbits. For such a band to live entirely on fish, 234 pounds of dressed fish would be required daily. This requirement could be met by 7 sturgeon of average size of 60 pounds or 150 black bass weighing 3 pounds each when caught.

This same band, if subsisting upon vegetal foods either collected wild or produced by agriculture would require daily about 75 to 100 pounds of pre-pared food. For instance, about 80 pounds of cornmeal or about 95 pounds of maple sugar or about 80 pounds of dried beans would suffice for this hypotheti-cal band, assuming for purposes of illustration that they ate only one kind of food at a time.

The aboriginal population of the Upper Great Lakes at the time of the white man's arrival was sparse, judged by modern standards. Although there are no precise figures available, an estimate of about 100,000 persons seems es-sentially correct. This is a substantial number of people when one considers that the estimated aboriginal population for all of North America north of Mexico was little more than one million persons. The Upper Great Lakes re-gion contained about 10 per cent of the population in the entire area at the time.

This book is the story of what happened to the region during the retreat of the glaciers and during the periods following. It is the history of man and his environment from about 11,000 B.C. to A.D. 1800.

The story admittedly is incomplete. The data for interpretation are few and new data, as they are discovered, may change many details and add many new ideas to the prehistory of the region. But here at least is an outline of what happened in the prehistoric Upper Great Lakes region, based on the informa-tion available in 1958.

About 18,000 years ago the climate of the whole world was much colder than now and the Upper Great Lakes region was buried under masses of ice hundreds and hundreds of feet thick. This was the climax of the Wisconsin glaciation, the last of a series of great continental glaciers. No large climatic change occurred until at least 13,000 years ago. After that time the climate became increasingly warmer and the glaciers eventually melted.

This glacial retreat in the Upper Great Lakes area began about 11,000 B.C., or shortly before. At first the retreat was slow and interrupted by temporary advances of the ice front. But after about 8500 B.C. deglaciation, or retreat of the ice, was very rapid. By 6000 B.C. the basins of the present Upper Great Lakes were entirely free of ice.

As the ice retreated northward, plants, shrubs, and trees moved into the region. This process is aptly described by the late Frère Marie-Victorin, who wrote as follows:

And now we imagine the aggressive types of the so-called Canadian spruce forest coming up North, striding over moraines and ice polished slopes, surrounding the nunataks and invading those secluded rock-gardens of the past. Indeed a great biological picture, this onward march, spread on the geological timescale! In America at least, there was no frowning Macbeth on the wall to watch Birnam woods coming up to Dunsinane. But nevertheless, on and on came the "moving groves."

First came those ever ready pioneers: the Black Spruce and the White Spruce, and the Balsam Fir, and the Larch, and later the stately pines. Then followed the Aspens and the Birches, the Alders and Viburnums. The sugar Maple took possession of the well drained moraines alongside the valleys, and the Hemlock fought its way among the deciduous trees. Meanwhile had come the wiry Grasses and the coarse Sedges, the legions of Goldenrods and Asters, [and] the hundreds after hundreds of herbaceous or shrubby plants.

As the vegetation spread northward in the wake of the retreating glaciers, the animals pushed northward following the vegetation.

First came the mammoths and mastodons, particularly the latter, and apparently with them were giant beaver, deer, elk, and caribou. In the Lake Huron basin there seem to have been whales, and perhaps walrus. The deer, elk, and caribou were present in the region after the mastodons had left it.

As the animals moved into the Upper Great Lakes area so did people—the Indians. First came the Paleo-Indians who used fluted points of chipped stone for the spearing of large animals such as mastodons. Next came the hunters with their lanceolate blades of Aqua-Plano style and the ancient Indians who worked the quartzite quarries in the northern part of the area. Then came the ancient boreal hunters with their woodworking tools of ground stone and the Old Copper Indians, who made many of their tools and weapons of copper and hunted the elk and barren-ground caribou.

By about 100 B.C., the era of the Indians who lived solely by hunting and fishing was at its end. New groups of Indians entering the region from the south brought with them new and revolutionary things such as agriculture and elaborate burial customs.

The new Indian mode of life in the southern part of the Upper Great Lakes region was based upon a combination of hunting and crude agriculture. The descendants of the early hunters who did not avail themselves of this new way of subsistence were the Indians along and beyond the northern periphery of the region where the habitat was suitable only for hunting and fishing.

These were the Indians and descendants of Indians who had moved north-ward in earlier times following the moving ecological zones to which they were adjusted. Even in recent times in northernmost Canada it has been possible to see Indians who represent a way of life that was present in all of the Upper Great Lakes region thousands of years ago. Probably such Indians are the actual descendants of some of the early hunters who lived in the Upper Great Lakes region in the millennia before 1000 B.C.

Of the first comers, the Paleo-Indians who used fluted points, we have no direct evidence other than finds of the points. No actual dwelling sites have been found in the Upper Great Lakes area. However, the distribution of the fluted-point finds provides an excellent clue to their age, suggesting the period from about 10,000 to 7000 B.C.

The period of fluted points is also the period of spruce-fir dominance in the forest cover and the period encompassing radiocarbon-dated mastodon re-mains. The information available suggests a functional relationship involving spruce-fir dominance in forest cover, mastodons, and fluted points. In the western United States the same kind of fluted point is associated with the hunting of mammoths in grasslands.

The Aqua-Plano Indians who lived by the shores of glacial and postglacial lakes and hunted with various kinds of lanceolate or leaf-shaped points seem to have occupied the region from about 7000 to about 5000 B.C. This was a time of declining spruce-fir and increasing pine in the forests of the southern portions of the region.

The Archaic Boreal Indians were in the Upper Great Lakes region by 5000

B.C. and the Indian carriers of the mysterious Old Copper culture that dominated the northern parts of the region existed from about 5000 to 1500 B.C.

The Old Copper Indians were the first fabricators of metal in either North or South America. They mined copper for the manufacture of tools and weapons and lived by hunting caribou, deer, elk, and probably bison. During the early part of this period the pine forest reached its peak in the western and southern parts of the region and began to decline as oak-chestnut forest and grasses increased.

The Archaic Boreal Indians were in the region from at least 5000 to 500 B.C. The Indian bearers of this culture lived by hunting as did their predecessors and contemporaries. What is distinctive about them in the Upper Great Lakes region is their use of ground- and polished-stone tools and weapons and their emphasis upon woodworking tools such as axes, gouges, and adzes. This woodworking assemblage seems to correlate with the development and climax of the deciduous forest in the Upper Great Lakes region. The climate during most of this period was the warmest it has ever been in the past 18,000 years.

From 500 to about 100 B.C. the region was occupied by groups of Early Woodland Indians. Although they still lived by hunting and fishing, they were the first people in the region to use pottery of fired clay and to erect burial mounds over their dead.

In the Middle Woodland period, from about 100 B.C. to A.D. 800, there was a cultural climax brought about by the arrival of the Hopewellian Indians from the valley of the Illinois River in Illinois. Elaborate burial mounds were erected over the dead. There was widespread trade and commerce with distant lands. There were artistic achievements that were never surpassed by later Indian occupants of the region. And agriculture had its beginnings.

In the Late Woodland period, from about A.D. 800 to 1600, there was an increasing differentiation of cultural groups in the region. During a particularly warm spell around 1000, some new groups of Indians entered the region from farther south via the Mississippi Valley and its tributaries, and other groups of Indians entered the region from the east. The Indians of this period made their living by hunting and farming.

The Indian tribes of the Upper Great Lakes region at the time of the arrival of Europeans in the seventeenth century were the Miami, Sauk, Fox, Potawatomi, Ottawa, Huron, Chippewa or Ojibwa, Menomini, and Winnebago. All of these tribes were products of cultural developments in the region during the Late Woodland period. Remnants of many of these tribes are still living in the Upper Great Lakes region at the present time.

REFERENCES

BROECKER and KULP, 1955; CRANE, 1956;
CRANE and GRIFFIN, 1958;
ERICSON, BROECKER, KULP, and WOLLIN, 1956;
GOODE, 1937; GRIFFIN, 1956; HANDLEY, 1953; HINSDALE, 1932;
HOUGH, 1958; KROEBER, 1939; MACALPIN, 1940;
MARIE-VICTORIN, 1940; MASON, 1958; QUIMBY, 1958;
SWANTON, 1952; ZIM and HOFFMEISTER, 1955.

2. DATING THE PAST

In attempting to reconstruct the prehistoric Indian mode of life and the changing environments of the past 13,000 years in the Upper Great Lakes region a chronological framework in which to place events in their proper sequence is necessary. Fortunately such a chronological framework can be constructed from the data of late Pleistocene or glacial geology, pollen analysis, and radiocarbon-dating.

For instance, an excellent geological clock of relative time is provided by the stratigraphic sequence of deposits made during the advance and retreat of the continental glaciers. Such things as moraines and outwash deposits produced by glaciation, the abandoned beaches, and the outlets and beds of glacial lakes ponded by the ice front at various positions, when ordered in the sequence in which they were formed, yield a relative chronology of geological events that can be correlated with archeological stages.

Another method of dating the past is by the analysis of plant pollen that falls to the earth or into lakes and ponds and is preserved in layers of soil or sediment, with the oldest at the bottom and the youngest on top. Quantitative analysis of different species of plants recorded by the fossil pollen, layer by layer, in peat or soil deposits enables the palynologist, or pollen expert, to reconstruct the vegetation that was growing in an area at the time the pollen was deposited at each level. A series of such layers with fossil pollen will show the succession of vegetation over a long period of time. Thus the palynologist can provide a relative chronology of the flora and, by inference, of the climate for a region.

The generalized sequence of flora in the Upper Great Lakes during the last twelve or thirteen thousand years is, first, a forest composed mainly of spruce and fir; next, a forest composed principally of pine; then a forest dominated by oak and pine; then an oak-hickory forest coeval with the maximum expansion of grasslands; and, finally, a forest in which oak and pine are dominant.

The climate inferred from these stages of flora is as follows: first, a period much colder than the present; next, a period of increasing warmth; then a warm period of long duration, most of which was much hotter than present; and, finally, a cooler period much like the present climate.

This floristic and climatic chronology can be correlated with the order of geological events and also with cultural activities discovered by means of archeological techniques.

Still another way of dating the past is provided by the radiocarbon-dating method developed by Dr. Willard Libby. This method determines the approximate age of organic substances by measuring with special apparatus the amount of carbon 14 they contain.

Carbon 14, a radioactive heavy form of carbon, is created constantly in the earth's upper atmosphere. It subsequently becomes part of the entire atmosphere and enters all living things. All living matter contains a constant proportion of carbon 14; thus when a plant or animal dies the percentage of carbon 14 in its tissues is known. And since carbon 14 then disintegrates at a known rate, the amount remaining at any given moment is proportional to the time elapsed since death.

By the use of proper equipment and technique in applying this principle, it is possible to measure the age of organic remains and the things with which they are associated. Thus the age of wood buried under a glacial deposit such as a moraine can be determined and the glacial stage represented by the moraine can be dated approximately. Similarly, the age of a piece of driftwood imbedded in a fossil beach can date the beach, the age of a mastodon tusk can fix the time of the animal's death, and a piece of charcoal from a prehistoric Indian campfire can provide the approximate date of an associated Indian village. It should be noted, however, that, for reasons inherent in the radiocarbon method, all radiocarbon dates should be considered approximations of absolute dates.

Radiocarbon dates usually are given as so many years before the present time, plus or minus a given number of years. These plus or minus years are a way of stating the statistical error of the radiocarbon measurement. For instance, a given radiocarbon date without error other than that due to radioactive process might be expressed as 1,000 years ago, plus or minus 40 years. This means there is about a 66 per cent probability that the sample measured has a true date, that is, any time between 1,040 and 960 years ago.

Doubling the statistical error increases the probability to about 96 per cent. Using the same sample for illustration there would be about 96 chances in 100 that the true date would fall at some time between 1,080 and 920 years ago. Tripling the error would provide virtual certainty that the true date of the sample would lie between 1,120 and 880 years ago.

Because of the size of the statistical error of a given radiocarbon date or because this error is doubled or tripled to increase probability, a number of radiocarbon dates of different events may overlap in time or even appear to reverse a stratigraphic sequence of events. In such instances one can use the known stratigraphy as the deciding factor and assume that the true date is either in the plus half or minus half of the statistical error, whichever best fits the stratigraphic situation.

As a matter of convenience the radiocarbon dates used in the following parts of this book are given without their statistical errors. Moreover, these dates have been changed to the conventional before Christ and anno Domini mode of presentation—1000 B.C. or A.D. 1066, for example. When a letter and number accompanies the date it is the catalogue designation of the institution that made the measurement and is provided here for the convenience of those persons particularly interested in radiocarbon dates.

By combining estimates of absolute time based on radiocarbon dates with the geological and pollen sequences, it is possible to construct a reasonably adequate chronological framework for the past 13,000 years in the Upper Great Lakes region.

The late glacial and postglacial geological events used in this 13,000-year timetable have been selected from the works of Drs. F. T. Thwaites, J H. Bretz, G. M. Stanley, J. L. Hough, J. H. Zumberge, W. N. Melhorn, and J. A. Elson.

The sequence of geological events in the Lake Michigan basin rests upon well-established field evidence and a reasonable supply of radiocarbon dates. The sequence of geological events in the Lake Huron basin is also based on good field evidence, but lacks an adequate supply of radiocarbon dates. The main difficulty in establishing a detailed geochronology for archeological purposes is the lack of proved correlations between events in these two lake basins prior to the Lake Algonquin stage. This is a critical problem which, because of lack of data, has not yet been solved.

There are at least three major theories of the correlation of pre-Algonquin geological events in the Lake Michigan and Lake Huron basins. Until new field evidence and/or more radiocarbon dates become available, all these correlations remain primarily different interpretations of essentially the same data. The chronological framework and events upon which this calendar is based are as follows:

Port Huron (*about 11,000–10,000 B.C.*)—The Port Huron moraine (see map, p. 20) marks the position of the front of the ice in this period. Part of this morainic system lies in northeastern Wisconsin, where it is buried beneath deposits of a later glacial advance. It extends across the northern part of lower

Fig. 1.—Map of the Upper Great Lakes region.

Michigan, where parts of it are beneath subsequent deposits, and then loops southward around the southern end of Lake Huron basin. It probably is coeval with a moraine across the Niagara Falls area.

In the Lake Michigan basin, the Glenwood stage of Lake Chicago—a glacial lake with a water plane 640 feet above present sea level and 60 feet above present Lake Michigan—is a correlative of the Port Huron moraine as well as of some earlier moraines. Specific correlations with lake stages in the Huron basin are in dispute.

The following radiocarbon dates indicate the general time levels toward the end of these events: Glenwood stage of Lake Chicago (W-161) 10,245 B.C.; Port Huron "gray till" deposits in northeastern Wisconsin (Y-147X) 9985 B.C.

Two Creeks Interstadial (about 10,000–9000 B.C.).—After 10,000 B.C. the ice retreated to positions north of the vicinity of the Straits of Mackinac. The opening of eastern outlets permitted the Huron and Michigan basins to be lowered considerably, perhaps nearly to sea level. The evidence for these events is as follows:

During this period a forest in the vicinity of Two Creeks, Wisconsin, stood at an elevation of about 580 feet above present sea level. At the end of the period, shortly before it was knocked down by an advancing glacier, the forest was flooded by rising waters of a glacial lake in the Michigan basin.

For a forest to stand at an elevation of 580 feet, the lake level in the Michigan basin had to be lowered by eastward drainage. There was no southern outlet low enough at this time, so the water in the Michigan had to drain into the Huron basin. For this to happen the ice would have had to be north of the vicinity of the present Straits of Mackinac.

The Huron basin could not have drained southward at this time, because there was no southern outlet as low as 580 feet. Therefore an eastern outlet must have drained the Huron basin.

Any available eastern outlet must have been free of glacial ice to permit drainage. Moreover, most possible eastern outlets would have drained the lake basins some hundreds of feet lower than 580 feet. And if the North Bay outlet had been one of those in use, the Huron and Michigan basins could have been drained nearly to sea level. This particular period of low water levels in the Huron and Michigan basins has been called the Bowmanville stage and Two Creeks low water stage.

It seems likely that during this stage the Lake Huron basin was connected to a marine invasion of the St. Lawrence Valley.

The following are some of the radiocarbon dates that indicate the termination of the Two Creeks Interstadial: Two Creeks forest bed (C-308, 365, 366, 536, 537) average 9450 B.C.; (Y-227) 9175 B.C.; (M-342) 8745 B.C.; (W-42, W-83 av.) 9415 B.C. Rise in water level at end of low-water stage (W-167) 8905 B.C.; (M-288a) 9245 B.C.

Valders Advance (about 9000–8500 B.C.)—About 9000 B.C. there was an advance of the ice sheet responsible for the deposits of reddish clay till known as Valders drift. The Valders deposits were mapped and identified in northeastern Wisconsin by Dr. F. T. Thwaites in 1943 and 1957, identified in western Michigan by Dr. J H. Bretz in 1951, and identified in the northern part of the southern peninsula of Michigan by Dr. W. N. Melhorn in 1954. East of Michigan the position of the Valders ice front is not known, but it or its correlative certainly covered the low eastern outlets at Kirkfield and North Bay, otherwise the high water levels of the glacial lakes contemporaneous with Valders could not have been attained.

In the Lake Michigan basin, the Calumet stage of Lake Chicago—a glacial lake with a water plane at 620 feet above present sea level—was coeval with Valders ice. Calumet shore features occur on the Valders red drift in Wisconsin and are deposited unconformably on top of Glenwood deposits in Michigan. Presumably the waters in the Lake Huron basin stood at 620 feet above modern sea level and connected with the Calumet level across the retreating ice in the northern part of lower Michigan and drained through the outlet at Chicago.

Although the Valders ice pushed south of the Port Huron ice position in the Michigan basin, it did not last long and did not produce many constructional features. For the most part, Valders drift is spread thinly on top of Port Huron deposits in Michigan and Wisconsin.

The reddish till of the Valders glacial advance lies not only on the Port Huron gray till but also on the lake plain of the Glenwood stage of glacial Lake Chicago and on the Two Creeks forest bed. Thus the stratigraphic position of Valders deposits proves that the Valders glacial advance was more recent than the Two Creeks Interstadial and the Port Huron glaciation.

The radiocarbon dates marking the termination of the Two Creeks Interstadial also date the inauguration of the Valders advance. A radiocarbon date marking the early retreat of the Valders ice is (C-630) 8725 B.C. A radiocarbon date that indicates the retreat of the Valders ice at a time probably later than the Calumet stage is (M-359) 8265 B.C.

Early Valders Retreat (around 8500–8000 B.C.).—The water level in the Lake Michigan basin dropped from the Calumet level as the Chicago outlet became lowered by erosion.

After a pause of unknown duration at about the 600-foot level, marking the Toleston stage, the water plane dropped still more to about 580 feet above present sea level. This low level is indicated by a post-Calumet and pre-Algonquin beach some 25 feet beneath the Algonquin level that was dis-covered in northern Michigan by Dr. J. H. Zumberge in 1955. Its level implies the use of an outlet at that time, temporarily ice-free, east of Georgian Bay.

The waters of both the Huron and Michigan basins stood at 580-foot level and the Valders ice front probably was just north of the straits of Mackinac.

This low-water stage seems to have been brief and probably was the result of an oscillation of the ice front perhaps in the vicinity of the Kirkfield outlet.

Middle Valders Retreat (about 8000–7000 B.C.).—The glacial ice still covered the eastern half of the Lake Superior basin and the northeastern portion of the Lake Huron basin.

Glacial Lake Algonquin, with a water plane 605 feet above present sea level, occupied the basins of Lake Michigan and Lake Huron. Shoreline and bottom deposits of glacial Lake Algonquin lie on top of Valders glacial deposits, thus proving that the Lake Algonquin stage was later than the Valders glacial advance.

Glacial Lake Algonquin probably began at about 8000 B.C., or slightly earlier, and ended about 7000 B.C., or somewhat earlier. Some probable post-Algonquin radiocarbon dates are (W-345) 7175 B.C.; (C-674) 6248 B.C.; and (M-288) 6395 B.C.

Late Valders Retreat (about 7000–6000 B.C.).—During the very late retreat of the Valders glacier, the Kirkfield outlet and possibly other eastern outlets became free of ice and the water plane in the Huron and Michigan basins dropped to successively lower levels. These lower stages—Wyebridge at 540 feet above present sea level, Penetang at 510 feet, Cedar Point at 493 feet, Payette at 465 feet, Sheguiandah at 416 feet, and Korah at 390 feet—were beneath the level of, and therefore more recent than, the Algonquin beach. Moreover, in the uplifted parts of the region these lower strand lines are nearly parallel to the Algonquin beach, thus proving that the water levels were lowered prior to the major upwarping of the area. A low beach in this series called the Minong was registered in the Lake Superior basin and may have been coeval with Payette or one of the lower level substages.

By the end of the stage the ice had left the Lake Superior basin and the North Bay outlet had become free of ice.

This stage can be dated approximately by a radiocarbon measurement (W-

345) of 7175 B.C. That it terminated about 6000 B.C. by the opening of the North Bay outlet is suggested from the following evidence. Between the time of the ice retreat from Lake Superior and the North Bay region and the disappearance of Lake Ojibwa-Barlow, a large glacial lake north of the Huron basin, about 2,000 years elapsed, according to the clay varve counts of Dr. Ernst Antevs. Since glacial Lake Ojibwa-Barlow had ended by about 4425 B.C. (W-136), the North Bay outlet area should have been free of ice about 2,000 years earlier, assuming a generally northward retreat of the glacier.

Terminal Glacial (about 6000–3000 B.C.).—With the opening of the North Bay outlet, the water plane in the Huron and Michigan basins dropped nearly to sea level. Lake Chippewa in the Lake Michigan basin stood at 230 feet above present sea level and Lake Stanley in the Huron basin had a water plane about 180 feet above present sea level. The water level in the Lake Superior basin also was lowered considerably.

Some radiocarbon datings of events during the Chippewa-Stanley stage of low water levels are (C-848) 4485 B.C.; (L-312) 4345 B.C.; (L-214) 3175 B.C.; and (M-290) 3045 B.C. Radiocarbon dates (Y-238) 2925 B.C.; (S-24) 2695 B.C.; and (S-25) 2655 B.C. are associated with events that are later than the Chippewa-Stanley stage.

Early Postglacial (about 3000–1500 B.C.).—The Nipissing stage, manifested by a postglacial lake in the Superior, Michigan, and Huron basins, had a water plane of 605 feet above present sea level. It was created by the closing of the North Bay outlet through postglacial upwarping of the land, presumably expanding from the release of the weight of the glacial ice that covered it at an earlier time. In some northern parts of the region the land rose more than 400 feet between the time of glacial Lake Algonquin and Lake Nipissing.

The surface water level of the Upper Great Lakes during the Nipissing stage was controlled by the levels of the outlets at Chicago and Port Huron, Michigan.

Some Nipissing stage radiocarbon dates are as follows: (Y-238) 2925 B.C.; (C-504) 1705 B.C.; (C-364) 1518 B.C.; (S-24) 2695 B.C.; and (S-25) 2655 B.C. Two significant post-Nipissing radiocarbon dates are (M-363) 965 B.C. and (C-608) 667 B.C.

ESTIMATED DATES	ADVANCES AND RETREATS OF GLACIAL ICE	LAKE STAGES
A.D. 1800 ↕ 500 B.C.	Recent postglacial	Post-Algoma stages
500 B.C. ↕ 1500 B.C.	Later postglacial	Lake Algoma stage
1500 B.C. ↕ 3000 B.C.	Early postglacial	Lake Nipissing stage
3000 B.C. ↕ 6000 B.C.	Terminal glacial	Lake Chippewa-Stanley stage
6000 B.C. ↕ 7000 B.C.	Late Valders retreat	Transition stages between glacial Lake Algonquin and lakes Chippewa-Stanley
7000 B.C. ↕ 8000 B.C.	Middle Valders retreat	Glacial Lake Algonquin stage
8000 B.C. ↕ 8500 B.C.	Early Valders retreat	Pre-Algonquin stages including Toleston
8500 B.C. ↕ 9000 B.C.	Valders Glacial Advance	Calument stage and its correlatives
9000 B.C. ↕ 10,000 B.C.	Two Creeks Interstadial	Two Creeks low water stage
10,000 B.C. ↕ 11,000 B.C.	Port Huron glacial advance	Glenwood stage and its correlatives

Fig. 2.—Calendar derived from geological events and radiocarbon measurements

Late Postglacial (about 1500–500 B.C.).—In the Upper Great Lakes region this period is manifested by the Algoma stage with a water plane 595 feet above present sea level. This stage was inaugurated by down-cutting of the Port Huron outlet and was terminated by further down-cutting of the same general outlet. Radiocarbon dates indicative of the latter part of this period are (M-363) 965 B.C. and (C-608) 667 B.C. A post-Algoma beach has a radiocarbon date (M-194) of 225 B.C.

Postglacial–Recent (500 B.C. to Present).—With the ending of the Algoma stage, the Upper Great Lakes closely approximated their present form with the only natural outlet at Port Huron, Michigan, through which they drain to the Lower Great Lakes via the Detroit River.

SUMMARY

The somewhat complicated outline of successive geological events and radiocarbon assessments of age presented above provides the basis for a kind of broad calendar to which one can relate the prehistoric Indian cultures and their changing environments in the Upper Great Lakes region.

A chart derived from this outline of geological events and radiocarbon dates is presented in Figure 2. This presentation with its estimates of absolute time is somewhat different from others. In many respects it is close to that provided by Hough but differs in ascribing greater antiquity to most of the geological events considered. Undoubtedly this calendar will be modified and refined by the discovery of new data and reinterpretation of the old. At this stage of Upper Great Lakes research there is still plenty of room for disagreement. But even in its preliminary or tentative form such a calendar is a necessary tool for the prehistorian and the paleogeographer interested in the Upper Great Lakes region.

REFERENCES | ANTEVS, 1928; BRETZ, 1951; BROECKER and KULP, 1955, 1956; CRANE, 1956; CRANE and GRIFFIN, 1958; DEEVEY and FLINT, 1957; ELSON, 1957; ERICSON, BROECKER, KULP, and WOLLIN, 1956; HOUGH, 1953, 1958; LEE, 1956; LIBBY, 1952; MELHORN, 1956; PRESTON, PERSON, and DEEVEY, 1955; SPAULDING, 1958; SPURR and ZUMBERGE, 1956; STANLEY, 1937, 1938, 1941, 1943, 1948; THWAITES, 1943; THWAITES and BERTRAND, 1957; ZUMBERGE, 1956; ZUMBERGE and POTZGER, 1956.

3. THE ARCHEOLOGY
OF ENVIRONMENT

Primitive cultures, especially those of hunting peoples, are much more dependent upon the physical qualities of environment than are the urban cultures of civilized peoples. Other factors being equal, the physical environment not only limits the culture of hunting peoples but may also be a determining factor in the form that the culture will take.

During most of the last 12,000 years the Upper Great Lakes area was the homeland of a succession of primitive hunting cultures manifesting traditions of the Paleo-Indian and Boreal Archaic stages.

These primitive Indian cultures must have been closely tied to their environments through the interaction of habitat and culture. Yet late glacial and postglacial geological data, as well as climatic information derived from analysis of fossil pollen, indicate that these Upper Great Lakes environments were constantly changing.

With these alterations of surroundings there must have been corresponding modifications in the cultures. Thus, in order to arrive at any reasonable understanding of the cultural archeology of the Upper Great Lakes region, it is first desirable to know the archeology of the physical environment.

In the following sections the archeology of environment will be briefly presented in terms of the geochronological periods outlined in the preceding chapter.

Port Huron Glacial Advance (11,000 to 10,000 B.C.).—During the Port Huron glacial advance, a period beginning some time after 11,000 B.C. and ending about 10,000 B.C., the glacial ice covered most of Ontario, much of northern Michigan, and a part of northeastern Wisconsin (Fig. 3).

Large glacial lakes with water planes much higher than at present occupied the basins of Lakes Michigan and Huron south of the ice front, but the Lake Superior basin was entirely covered by ice. West and northwest of the Lake

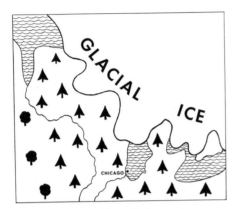

Fig. 3.—Upper Great Lakes region at time of Port Huron glacial advance between 11,000 and 10,000 B.C.

Fig. 4.—Upper Great Lakes region at time of Two Creeks Interstadial between 10,000 and 9000 B.C.

Superior basin there was a tremendous glacial lake, Lake Agassiz, which occupied parts of western Minnesota, eastern North Dakota, and most of Manitoba.

The ice-free portions of the land in the Upper Great Lakes region were covered by forest of spruce and fir possibly separated from the glacial front by a narrow strip of tundra. The climate of this period was certainly much colder and probably wetter than the present.

The animals living in the ice-free portions of the land included mammoths, mastodons, giant beavers, deer, elk, and barren-ground caribou. Sea mammals inhabiting the glacial lakes ponded by the ice were whales of several species and walruses.

Two Creeks Interstadial (10,000 to 9000 B.C.).—With the retreat of the Port Huron ice to a position north of the Straits of Mackinac, the Huron and Michigan basins were ice-free (Fig. 4). So were parts at least of the Superior basin; for Lake Agassiz drained eastward into it at this time and was considerably lowered, if not temporarily dry. The ice east of the Huron basin had retreated in a northerly direction, opening low outlets which drained to the Lake Ontario basin and the St. Lawrence River Valley. The western Great Lakes, by draining through these newly opened outlets, were considerably lower, probably some hundreds of feet, than their previous levels. The era of greatly reduced lakes in the Michigan and Huron basins comprises the Two Creeks low-water stage.

During this stage much more land would have been available for Paleo-Indian occupancy than before. The lowered water planes exposed former lake bottom lands.

The drainage of all the Upper Great Lakes at this period was eastward, probably to an arm of the ocean in the St. Lawrence Valley. Lake Agassiz drained to the Superior basin, which in turn drained to either the Michigan or Huron basin. The Michigan basin drained to the Huron basin, and the Huron basin drained to the ocean through one of the outlets to the east, probably at North Bay.

The land was covered by a forest in which spruce and fir were dominant. Other trees known to have been present were tamarack, pine, oak, ash, linden, and cedar.

The climate seems to have been cooler and probably moister than that of the present time.

The animals living in the region included mastodons, giant beavers, deer, elk, and barren-ground caribou. Sea mammals were whales and walruses, which in small numbers may have entered the Lake Huron basin from the ocean by way of the Ottawa River and the North Bay channel.

Valders Glacial Advance (9000 to 8500 B.C.).—The Two Creeks Intersta-dial and low-water stages were terminated by the advance of the Valders glacier. Once again the ice moved southward, pushing over the forests, filling most or all of the Lake Superior basin, crossing the Straits of Mackinac to cover northern Michigan and parts of northeastern Wisconsin, and blocking the outlets to the sea east of the Huron basin (Fig. 5).

The water levels in the ice-free parts of lake basins dammed by the glacier rose to high levels. The water plane in the Lake Michigan basin, for instance, rose to at least 620 feet above present sea level. Lake Agassiz, with its low eastern outlet blocked by ice in the Lake Superior basin, rose to its old beach levels and drained southward to the Mississippi River.

On and on came the Valders ice, loaded with red clay and rock debris picked up in the Lake Superior region. In the Lake Michigan basin the ice reached as far south as Milwaukee, Wisconsin, and Muskegon, Michigan.

Shortly after reaching its maximum spread, the Valders ice sheet began to retreat rapidly. The depositional features left by the melting ice are all rel-atively thin and indicative of a rapid retreat. And the deposits left by the Valders ice are all easily recognizable because of their red coloring.

The ice-free portions of the land still maintained a forest dominated by spruce and fir trees, and this forest seems to have extended right up to the ice margins. The climate remained cool and moist, but was getting progressively warmer than it had been.

The inventory of animal life was the same as was mentioned previously. Mastodons were still abundant and there were at least a few whales in the waters of the Huron basin.

Valders Retreat (8500 to 7000 B.C.).—As the Valders ice retreated, the Huron and Michigan basins were joined across the ice front, first at a level of at least 620 feet, then at 580 feet, and finally at 605 feet above the present sea level. The 580-foot level may represent an oscillation of ice blocking the Kirkfield outlet east of the Huron basin. In any event the longest part of this segment of the Valders retreat is the Lake Algonquin stage. Lake Algonquin was a glacial lake in the Huron and Michigan basins with a water plane 605 feet above present sea level, discharging at Chicago and Port Huron (Fig. 6).

Just prior to the Lake Algonquin stage, the ice had retreated from northeastern Wisconsin, allowing Later Lake Oshkosh, a small glacial lake, to drain to extinction. The western half of the Superior basin was also free of ice by this time, allowing Lake Agassiz to drain eastward again.

During the time of Lake Algonquin, the ice extended from north of Lake Agassiz to the eastern half of the Superior basin, across the northeastern part of the Huron basin, and at least as far south as the Kirkfield outlet east of Georgian Bay.

The land areas were still covered with forests in which spruce and fir were dominant and the climate was still cooler and moister than at present. The forest-dwelling animals included mastodons, deer, elk, barren-ground caribou, and probably giant beaver. Whales still seem to have lived in the waters of the Lake Huron basin.

Late Valders Retreat (7000 to 6000 B.C.).—About 7000 B.C. or shortly before, the Valders ice retreated from the Kirkfield outlet east of Georgian Bay and the waters of Michigan and Huron basins drained eastward at successively falling levels (Fig. 7). First came the Wyebridge stage at 540 feet above present sea level, next the Penetang at 510 feet, then the Cedar Point stage at 493 feet, followed by the Payette level at 465 feet, and finally lower stages like the Minong, Sheguiandah, and Korah.

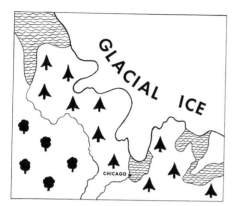

Fig. 5.—Upper Great Lakes region at time of Valders glacial advance between 9000 and 8500 B.C.

Fig. 6.—Upper Great Lakes region during Valders retreat and glacial Lake Algonquin, about 8500 to 7000 B.C.

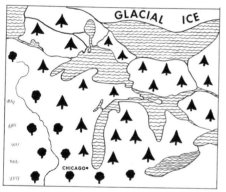

Fig. 7.—Upper Great Lakes region during Late Valders retreat and the falling water levels that followed glacial Lake Algonquin, 7000 to 6000 B.C.

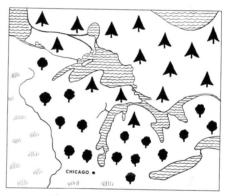

Fig. 8.—Upper Great Lakes region at the time of the Chippewa-Stanley stage, about 6000 to 3000 B.C.

During this period the ice retreated from the North Bay outlet and from the northeastern part of the Lake Superior basin. Lake Agassiz, still a large glacial lake, drained eastward into the Superior basin, and northeast of Lake Superior a new glacial lake was forming between the height of land and the ice front.

In this period the composition of the forests was changing. Spruce and fir were waning while pine was increasing.

Animal life in the southern half of the region was changing too. The mastodons were disappearing, either becoming extinct or moving northward.

Among the animals remaining were the deer, elk, and barren-ground caribou. A few whales continued to inhabit the waters.

Terminal Glacial (6000 to 3000 B.C.).—By the beginning of this period the ice front had retreated to a point near Cochrane, Ontario. Between the ice front and the height of land there was a tremendous glacial lake called Ojibwa-Barlow (Fig. 7). It lay east of Lake Agassiz and north of the Lake Huron basin, and drained southward either into the Huron basin or into the Ottawa River.

Lake Agassiz, still a glacial lake, but probably somewhat reduced in size, drained eastward into the Superior basin.

The Superior, Huron, and Michigan basins had extraordinarily low water levels. Lake Stanley in the Huron basin had a water plane about 180 feet above present sea level. This was 400 feet beneath the modern level of Lake Huron. Lake Chippewa in the Michigan basin had a water plane of 230 feet and was 350 feet below the level of modern Lake Michigan (Fig. 8). Lake Chippewa drained to Lake Stanley through a long river that passed through the present Straits of Mackinac. Lake Stanley drained to the ocean via the North Bay outlet and the Ottawa River. Lake Superior, lowered in level some hundreds of feet, drained to the level of the sill in the St. Mary's River and may have drained lower through northeastern outlets to Lake Ojibwa-Barlow.

By about the middle of this period the ice front in the vicinity of Cochrane, Ontario, retreated, allowing Lake Ojibwa-Barlow to drain northward and vanish shortly thereafter.

The forest cover of the land surrounding the lakes was changing in response to an increasingly warmer and drier climate. During the first half of the period pines achieved dominance of the forest from Minnesota to southern Michigan as the spruce-fir zone migrated northward. With the dominance of pine came an increase in the expansion of grasslands, particularly in the western parts of the area and between Lake Agassiz and the Superior basin, although on the northern periphery of the region there was a brief interval during which spruce-fir increased.

In the latter half of the period the pine dominance began to give way before the expansion of hardwood forest with oak and chestnut, and the grasslands increased still more their encroachments upon the forests. By the end of this period the climate was hotter and drier than that of today. Except perhaps in the far north, the mastodons seem to have left the region. But

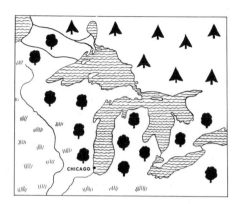

Fig. 9.—Upper Great Lakes region in early postglacial times during the Nipissing stage, about 3000 to 1500 B.C.

some whales were to be found. Deer, elk, and barren-ground caribou were among the animals still dwelling in the area. There is some evidence suggesting the presence of bison in the western parts of the region during part of this period. Dogs of several kinds made their first appearance in association with primitive Indian cultures.

Early Postglacial (3000 to 1500 B.C.).—Although the glacier had retreated from the Upper Great Lakes area, its former presence was being manifested in a peculiar way. The land, which had been compressed by the tremendous weight of the ice, had been rising relatively rapidly for less than 3,000 years. In places north of the hinge lines this rise amounted to about 400 feet, suggesting a rate of upwarping greater than one foot every ten years. The upwarping raised the North Bay outlet, thus causing the waters of the Upper Great Lakes to rise to levels controlled by outlets at Chicago and Port Huron, and for the first time the waters of the Huron, Superior, and Michigan basins were merged into one great lake. This was the Nipissing stage with a water plane 605 feet above present sea level (Fig. 9).

South of the upwarped areas the high waters of the Lake Nipissing reached the levels they had attained 5,000 years earlier. Many places that had long been dry land were once again under water and in the north some large areas were under water for the first time since the ice had left.

During the Nipissing times the forests dominated by oak and hickory achieved their maximum extension northward. This also was the period of the greatest expansion of the grasslands. It was also the time of the hottest and driest climate known in North America during the last 20,000 or more years.

Deer and elk were among the animals living in the region during the Nipissing epoch. Whales may have lasted until this period, as remains have been found inclosed in a Nipissing beach in Michigan.

Postglacial (1500 to 500 B.C.).—The waters of Lake Nipissing were lowered by down-cutting of their outlets. For a time between 1500 and 500 B.C. the levels in the Huron and Michigan basins were stabilized with a water plane at 595 feet above present sea level. This is the Algoma stage.

Around 1000 B.C. there was an abnormally cold period but it did not last for many years.

The northern lands continued to rise, but at a much slower rate than previously. The upwarping since Nipissing times has been about 80 to 100 feet in some places.

After the Algoma stage the Upper Great Lakes region took on its modern appearance and the flora and fauna were essentially as they existed at the time the European explorers arrived.

REFERENCES

ANTEVS, 1928; BRETZ, 1951; BROECKER and KULP, 1955; CRANE, 1956; CRANE and GRIFFIN, 1958; DEEVEY and FLINT, 1957; ELSON, 1957; ERICSON, BROECKER, KULP, and WOLLIN, 1956; GRIFFIN, 1956; HANDLEY, 1953; HOUGH, 1953, 1958; LIBBY, 1952; MACALPIN, 1940; MELHORN, 1956; PRESTON, PERSON, and DEEVEY, 1955; SHARP, 1953; SPURR and ZUMBERGE, 1956; STANLEY, 1937, 1938, 1941, 1943, 1948, 1953; THWAITES, 1943; THWAITES and BERTRAND, 1957; ZUMBERGE, 1956; ZUMBERGE and POTZGER, 1956.

4. MASTODONS AND MEN

Who were the first settlers of the Upper Great Lakes region? At the present time direct archeological proof is lacking. Nevertheless, a good circumstantial case can be made that they were Paleo-Indians who used spears pointed with fluted blades of chipped stone.

Fluted points are unique and easily recognized because they have longitudinal grooves or channels. There are several varieties of such points.

Clovis fluted points (named for a site in New Mexico) are the type most commonly found in the Upper Great Lakes region. They are lanceolate shapes with parallel or slightly convex sides and concave bases. They range in length from one and one-half inches to about six inches. The longitudinal flutes or grooves sometimes extend almost the full length of the blade but usually reach no more than halfway from base to tip. The flutes are most often produced by the removal of multiple flakes. Most Clovis points are fluted on both faces, but some are fluted on only one face. Generally the basal parts of fluted points have been dulled and smoothed by some sort of grinding (Fig. 10).

In the West, Clovis fluted points were used by Paleo-Indians who hunted mammoths (elephants) that lived in the lush grasslands prevailing in that region long ago. There is some evidence indicating that the western Clovis points belong to a period prior to 8000 B.C., and most archeologists have assumed that the fluted points found in the eastern half of North America are as old as those found in the West.

Although large numbers of fluted points have been found in the eastern portions of the United States, they have come from few known sites, which, with one exception, have not yet been radiocarbon-dated.

More than one hundred fluted points have been found in the Upper Great Lakes region. Unfortunately no sites attributable to the Paleo-Indians who used these instruments have been discovered so far. All of these points were surface finds.

Fortunately the distribution of these fluted points and the specific places

Fig. 10.—Fluted spearpoint of Clovis type from Chicago area

in which they were found can be related to radiocarbon-dated geological events in such a way as to provide a generally dated period during which the Paleo-Indians who made them lived.

For instance, certain areas covered by glacial ice or by waters of a glacial lake were inaccessible to the Paleo-Indians. These first settlers could only have lived and hunted in regions open to them. Local areas of the Upper Great Lakes did become available to these Paleo-Indians as the ice retreated and the glacial lake waters receded. And by knowing where these first Paleo-Indians were at various times, it is possible to estimate the period during which they lived and hunted in the region.

Fluted points have never been found in Michigan north of the Port Huron moraine, a system of glacial deposits that indicate the front of the glacial ice as late as about 10,000 B.C. So the Paleo-Indians who used fluted points could have been, and presumably were, inhabiting available areas south of the glacial ice at this time.

Some fluted points have been found in places on an old bed (Glenwood stage) of glacial Lake Chicago that was in existence until about 10,000 B.C. Therefore these particular points were left there some time after 10,000 B.C.

Other fluted points have been found in Wisconsin north of the southern limits of Valders till—reddish clay glacial deposits that were left by melting ice about 9000 B.C. These points could not have been placed where they were found until some time after the retreat of the Valders glacier, thus they date from a time later than about 9000 B.C.

Two fluted points have been found on an old bed (Calumet stage) of

Fig. 11.—Mastodon, a type of elephant now extinct

glacial Lake Chicago that was coeval with the Valders glacier of 9000 B.C. These points, therefore, would have reached the spots where they were found some time after about 9000 B.C.

Some fluted points found on the old bed of Later Lake Oshkosh, a glacial lake in Wisconsin formed by the retreating Valders glacier, must have been deposited after about 8500 B.C., the approximate terminal date of Later Lake Oshkosh.

No fluted points have been found on the old bed of glacial Lake Algonquin, but fluted points have been found on the landward side of fossil beaches of this glacial lake. Since the Lake Algonquin stage ended by about 7000 B.C., fluted points must be earlier than this date.

The distribution of these fluted points and their relationships to radio-carbon-dated geological events, as well as evidence gleaned elsewhere, indicate that the Paleo-Indians who used fluted points were in the Upper Great Lakes region in the period from about 10,000 to about 7000 b.c. This is also the period in which mastodons were most abundant in the region.

Mastodons, like mammoths, were members of the elephant family and are now extinct. Those in the Upper Great Lakes area were similar in size and appearance to extant Indian elephants but lower and longer in relative proportions, and they probably were hairy (Fig. 11).

Mastodons, unlike mammoths, were browsers. They ate leaves, stems, and twigs. They lived in forests and seem to have been most concentrated around swamps and the lowland areas near streams, rivers, and lakes.

The distribution of mastodon remains in the Upper Great Lakes region indicates that they are all more recent than the maximum or climax of the last glacial period. Some mastodon remains have been found in deposits on top of an old lake bed (Glenwood stage) of glacial Lake Chicago that was abandoned about 10,000 b.c. Such remains, being in place on top of the old lake bed, must date from a period more recent than 10,000 b.c.

Other mastodon remains have been found on top of a later bed of glacial Lake Chicago (Calumet stage) that was abandoned slightly after 9000 b.c. These particular mastodon remains, therefore, must represent mastodons that were living some time after 9000 b.c.

Three mastodons found in or near the Upper Great Lakes region have been radiocarbon-dated by the University of Michigan. One of these found in Noble County, Indiana, had a radiocarbon date of 10,676 b.c., another from Madison County, Ohio, has a date of 7645 b.c., and one from Lenawee County, Michigan, had a radiocarbon date of 7613 b.c.

Thus the evidence from distribution and geological situations as well as radiocarbon dates shows that mastodons lived in the Upper Great Lakes region during the period from about 10,000 b.c. to 7000 b.c., apparently the same period during which the Paleo-Indians who used fluted points lived in the area (Fig. 12).

Despite the lack of direct evidence, these Paleo-Indians using fluted points must have been elephant (mastodon) hunters. The western Paleo-Indians who used fluted points were elephant (mammoth) hunters par excellence and it seems inconceivable that similar Paleo-Indians dwelling in the Upper Great Lakes during the time of the mastodons would not also be elephant-hunters. The fluted point attached to a wooden shaft and used as a spear would have been an ideal weapon for primitive elephant-hunters.

The spear tipped with a fluted point was streamlined. The split shaft fitted

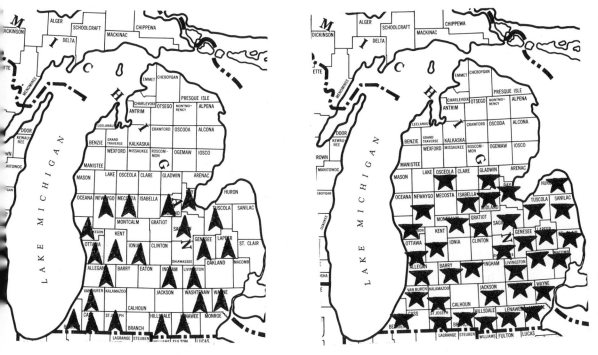

Fig. 12.—Distribution of fluted points and mastodon remains in Michigan. Map at LEFT *shows counties where fluted points have been found. Map at* RIGHT *shows counties where mastodon remains have been found.*

into the flutings of the large stone point and was fastened by bindings around the ground portions of the lower sides of the point. There were no barbs or projections. Such a spear could be thrust through flesh, fat, and muscle and withdrawn and thrust again. Such a spear could go through narrow interstices between ribs or other bones. Also it could be long enough and strong enough to reach the vital organs that were a considerable distance from the exterior surface of the animal.

No other type of aboriginal spear point in North America seems as well suited for elephant-hunting as the large fluted point. It may therefore be concluded that the Clovis fluted points were elephant points and that the Upper Great Lakes Paleo-Indians who used fluted points were mastodon-hunters.

These Paleo-Indians had to make their living by hunting, because no other mode of subsistence was possible in the region at this time. Among the animals available to them were not only the mastodons, but also the giant beaver, deer, elk, and caribou. Any spear capable of killing a mastodon could easily have dispatched these smaller animals. But the hunting of mastodons must have presented special problems. It seems likely that the animal was weakened in some way—by hamstringing, snaring of feet, or miring in a swamp—before being attacked by hunters. With the quarry at a disadvantage, five or six hunters could spear him through the rib cage or belly. The mastodon would have to be butchered at the place of the kill. Even a small one would have been too heavy to carry away intact.

The first settlers of the Upper Great Lakes were by necessity nomadic. In order to obtain food, shelter, and clothing by hunting, they would have had to range over wide areas of the region. Their shelters probably were made of sapling poles covered with bark or skins.

They wore clothing made of animal skins and made tools and weapons of chipped stone and probably bone and wood.

Nothing is yet known of their burial customs or of their physical appearance because no skeletal remains have been found.

What is known of their culture and habitat suggests that these Paleo-Indians were socially organized in small bands, and that political and religious institutions were lacking. Probably they possessed simple religious ideas based upon awe of nature, attempts to control their luck in hunting, and philosophical adjustments to their habitat.

At the time these Paleo-Indians lived in the Upper Great Lakes region the environment was much different from what it has been in recent times. A large continental-type glacier was present in the region throughout the period. This glacier, in retreat at about 10,000 B.C., advanced southward about 9000 B.C., then receded northward, leaving the northeast shore of Lake Superior about 7000 B.C.

The Lake Michigan and Lake Huron basins at first had high water levels. In the Lake Michigan basin, the surface water was 60 feet above its present level. With retreat of the glacier, low eastern outlets became available and the water levels in the lake basins were lowered some hundreds of feet by drainage. Then with the advance of the glacier and the subsequent closing of the low eastern outlets by ice, the water levels rose again. In the Lake Michigan basin the surface water stood at least 40 feet above its present level. During the final retreat of the glacier the surface water levels in the Huron and Michigan basins became stabilized for a long time at a level 25 feet above the present one.

The climate was colder and moister than that of modern times. The forests were dominated by spruce and fir trees. The animals that lived in the forests included the mastodons, giant beaver, deer, elk, and caribou. In the Lake Huron basin there seemed to have been whales and walruses, probably in very small numbers.

By the end of the period, about 7000 B.C., the climate was getting warmer. The continental glacier was receding rapidly and the spruce-fir forest was waning as pine trees advanced their hold over the land. The mastodons were disappearing too, either becoming extinct or moving northward in decreased numbers.

With the disappearance of the spruce-fir forests and mastodons, fluted points also disappeared. Perhaps some of the Paleo-Indians who used fluted points went northward, following the spruce-fir forest and the dwindling supply of mastodons. Others remaining in their old areas underwent cultural change in response to changes of habitat and the arrival of other Indians with a different technological tradition.

Whatever the cause, the cultural stage based on fluted points and related to mastodons and the spruce-fir forest ended by about 7000 B.C. and was succeeded by the Aqua-Plano stage of ancient Indian culture in the Upper Great Lakes region.

REFERENCES CRANE, 1956; CRANE and GRIFFIN, 1958; GRIFFIN, 1956; HANDLEY, 1953; MACALPIN, 1940; MASON, 1958; QUIMBY, 1958a; WORMINGTON, 1957.

5. LANCEOLATE POINTS AND
FOSSIL BEACHES

The Aqua-Plano groups of Paleo-Indians lived in the Upper Great Lakes area from about 7000 to about 4500 B.C. The Aqua-Plano tradition is manifested by lanceolate points often found in association with fossil beaches and water planes of glacial and ancient postglacial lakes (Figs. 13, 14).

These lanceolate points, formerly called Yuma, are now designated by specific type names, such as Plainview, Milnesand, Eden, Angostura, Browns Valley, Scottsbluff, and others. These point types and some additional ones seem to have been various expressions of a common tradition that has been called "Plano" in the West.

In the Plains region Plano points have been found associated with remains of bison, including bison species now extinct. The Plano tradition in the West represents an ancient hunting stage of Indian culture that followed an earlier stage manifested by the Paleo-Indians who used large fluted points and hunted kinds of elephants now extinct.

The situation in the Upper Great Lakes region is similar to that in the Plains. The Plano tradition is later than the fluted-point tradition. But since the lake region sites and Plano points are generally found in association with fossil beaches and water planes, it seems appropriate to use the term Aqua-Plano to designate the near-Plano tradition in the Upper Great Lakes area.

Most of the Aqua-Plano points found in the Upper Great Lakes region have been surface finds. There are, however, some excavated sites in the northern parts of the area (Fig. 15).

The westernmost of these sites in the basin of glacial Lake Agassiz is the Browns Valley site described by Dr. A. E. Jenks some twenty years ago. This site, located in Traverse County, Minnesota, consisted of a burial and stone tools and weapons placed in a grave pit dug into a gravel ridge, prior to the development of a humus or soil layer.

The gravel ridge was formed as a gravel bar in the southern outlet of Lake Agassiz and any burial in this ridge probably is later than any stage of Lake Agassiz that drained southward.

Lake Agassiz last drained southward during the time of the Valders glacial advance, about 9000 B.C., and continued to do so until the retreating glacier opened lower eastern outlets about 8000 B.C. or slightly later, permitting Lake Agassiz to drain eastward into the Superior basin. Thus the Browns Valley site should date from a period somewhat later than about 8000 B.C. On the basis of available evidence it seems likely that the Browns Valley find dates sometime between 7000 and 5000 B.C.

Fig. 13.—Aqua-Plano point of chipped quartzite from Kewaunee county, Wisconsin.

The skeleton in the Browns Valley grave was that of an adult male who was long-headed with a broad face. Accompanying the skeleton were the following: red ocher coloring; two small sandstone polishers; a flat stone, and six lanceolate, or leaf-shaped, points, three of which show definite parallel-flaking. There was also basal-smoothing on two of the blades with parallel-flaking and on two of the blades with less regular flaking.

Jenks also reported surface finds of other Plano points in Minnesota, including one made of quartzite.

Dr. John Elson has reported the presence of lanceolate points of the Plainview and Agate Basin types distributed around the periphery of Lake Agassiz II (a stage of this lake that lasted from around 8000 to about 3000 B.C.): This distribution indicates that Indians using lanceolate points lived along the shores of Lake Agassiz in some period later than 8000 B.C. and earlier than 3000 B.C.

Other surface finds of Aqua-Plano points in geological situations that date them as being more recent than about 8000 B.C. have been made in Wisconsin north of the southern limits of the last glacial advance and in the western part of the Lake Superior basin on the periphery of the old lake bed in the vicinity of Fort William, Ontario. Some of the points found near Fort William are made of taconite and show oblique parallel-flaking.

About 25 miles northeast of Fort William near Pass Lake, Ontario, in the

Fig. 14.—Some Aqua-Plano spearpoints

Thunder Cape region, there is an important archeological site excavated and described by Richard S. MacNeish. The Brohm site, as it is called, contained Aqua-Plano artifacts in the upper nine inches of pebble and clay beach deposits that were overlaid by deposits of humus. The artifacts were in the beach gravels before the humus zones developed on top of the gravels. This situation suggests that in ancient times Indians lived near the water's edge on top of the beach gravels very shortly after the deposition of the beach. Thus a determination of the age of the beaches gives a good clue to the age of the human occupation of these beaches.

Because of postglacial tilting of northern lands these beaches at the Brohm site are now 224 to 230 feet above the level of Lake Superior. At this elevation these beaches must represent the Lake Minong stage, a period of low water levels in the Superior basin and probably the first lake stage to be registered in the entire Superior basin. The reasons are as follows.

According to George M. Stanley, glacial geologist, the elevation of the highest of a continuous series of Minong stage beaches at the southwest end of the Isle Royale is 83 feet above Lake Superior and their angle of tilt is 2.6

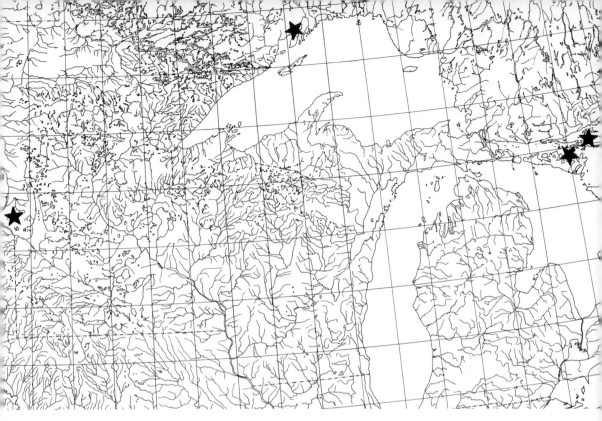

Fig. 15.—Map showing location of excavated sites that contributed to knowledge of Aqua-Plano culture

feet per mile along a line bearing N. 22° E. Projecting this water plane from southwestern Isle Royale 55 miles along a line bearing about N. 22° E. to the Brohm site, the anticipated elevation of the Minong strand would be 226 feet above Lake Superior, a perfect correlation between the upper part of the Minong series on Isle Royale and what must be the upper part of the Minong series at the Brohm site, where it ranges from 224 to 230 feet above Lake Superior.

What is the age of the Minong beach?

On the east shore of Lake Superior in the vicinity of Montreal River, the Minong beach is the first postglacial beach to be registered, but farther south on the east coast at Goulais it is about fifth beach stage in the series following Lake Algonquin and its correlatives. This position places the time of the Minong beach early in the Chippewa-Stanley stage of the Upper Great Lakes, or late in the perceding period, and suggests a date on the order of 7000 to 6000 B.C. for the occupancy of the Brohm site.

The Brohm-site people had blades, spearpoints, scrapers, and bifaced choppers made of chipped stone, mostly taconite, but also some flint and quartzite.

37

Many of the Brohm-site points were lanceolate or leaf-shaped, with parallel- or ripple-flaking. At least six of these points were of the type called "Plain-view," and others resemble the Milnesand type.

The Paleo-Indians who occupied the Brohm site were people who lived by hunting. They made tools and weapons similar to those of other Paleo-Indians living at about the same time in other areas. However, the Brohm-site people made most of their tools and weapons of taconite, a stone that was obtained locally (Fig. 16). They also used some quartzite, which might have been acquired elsewhere.

Many miles east and south in the northern part of Lake Huron basin there are ancient Indian sites where quartzite was the predominant material used for making tools and weapons.

One of these sites, a quarry, workshop, and habitation area near the town of Sheguiandah, Ontario, on the eastern end of Manitoulin Island, was excavated by Thomas E. Lee.

The geological details of the Sheguiandah site are complicated and subject to some disagreement. However, it seems obvious that the Sheguiandah site was under ice during the Valders glacial advance and for some time after the retreat of the ice it was beneath the waters of Lake Algonquin. The Sheguiandah site, therefore, could have been occupied only in the period preceding the Valders advance or in some period following Lake Algonquin stage, or perhaps in both periods.

If the Sheguiandah site were occupied only in some period after the Lake Algonquin stage—the theory accepted here—then the earliest occupancy would be a time when the Lake Algonquin waters had been lowered at least 300 feet and probably about 350 feet, a proposition necessitated by the position and present elevation of the site.

Upon this basis the earliest possible occupation of the Sheguiandah site would have been in the falling water stages following glacial Lake Algonquin and Lake Payette, but before the Lake Stanley stage, which began about 6000 B.C.

One radiocarbon date from the site, 7175 B.C., seems somewhat early, but this date could be as late as 6425 B.C., if no error other than statistical error due to radioactive process were involved. Some time between 7000 and 6000 B.C. seems to be a reasonable estimate for the earliest occupancy of the Sheguiandah site.

The use of the Sheguiandah site may have continued into the Nipissing

Fig. 16.—Artifacts made of taconite from Brohm site, Lake Superior area.
UPPER LEFT *is fragment of blade with diagonal flaking;* UPPER RIGHT *is
scraper; and* LOWER LEFT *and* RIGHT *are graving tools.*

stage of the Upper Great Lakes, about 3000 to 1500 B.C., because the area of
site occupancy rather abruptly terminates at the Nipissing water plane, which
at this place is about 70 feet above the present level of Lake Huron.

The occupation levels of the Sheguiandah site have produced a tremendous
quantity of bifaced blade or scraper-like objects of quartzite that exhibit many
variations in shape, size, and chipping or flaking. The points associated with
the site are usually of chipped quartzite. Some of these are of Aqua-Plano
types, whereas others resemble the notched and stemmed forms of the Boreal
Archaic and Old Copper cultures. Such a range of point types seems in keeping with periods of site occupancy between about 7000 and 1500 B.C.

On the Ontario mainland about 20 miles east of the Sheguiandah site near
the village of Killarney is the George Lake site excavated by Emerson F.
Greenman. This too is a quarry and workshop site where the Indians utilized
the abundant white quartzite. Among the materials found at the site were
biface choppers, large ovate and quadrangular blades, perforators, semilunar
blades, a water-worn scraper-graver tool, and three Aqua-Plano points.

These cultural materials were associated with a fossil beach 297 feet above the present level of Lake Huron. These materials were on the beach and in the upper parts of the beach. Moreover, according to Dr. Greenman, some of the artifacts were water-worn, as if they had been subjected to wave action.

The fossil beach associated with the George Lake site is about 180 feet beneath the anticipated water plane of Lake Algonquin and correlates with the beach series of the Cedar Point stage, according to Dr. George M. Stanley. Since the Lake Algonquin beach is not registered in the Killarney hills, this area was covered by glacial ice until a time later than the Lake Algonquin stage.

The site would have been covered by waters of a glacial lake during the Wyebridge and Penetang stages, but would have been available for occupancy in the Cedar Point stage.

Thus the earliest possible occupancy of the George Lake site would have been in the period following Lake Algonquin, but preceding Lake Chippewa-Stanley, or sometime between about 7000 and 6000 B.C. The association of the cultural remains with the fossil beach suggests that the earliest occupancy of the site was in this period.

The various Paleo-Indians who left the cultural remains indicative of the Aqua-Plano tradition seem to have lived in the Upper Great Lakes region sometime between about 7000 and 4500 B.C.

This time span embraces the post–Algonquin Lake stages—Wyebridge, Penetang, Cedar Point, Payette, Minong, Sheguiandah, and Korah—as well as the first half of the Chippewa-Stanley stage.

It was a period of general glacial retreat, falling water levels, and increasing warmth of climate. The Valders ice still in eastern Lake Superior basin and in parts of the northern Lake Huron basin at the beginning of the period had retreated to northernmost Ontario by the end of the period.

The lakes in the Huron, Michigan, and Superior basins were considerably reduced in area because of the falling water levels produced by low eastern outlets uncovered by the retreating ice. There were, however, two additional great lakes of enormous size. In the northwest lay glacial Lake Agassiz whose waters drained eastward to the Superior basin, and to the north and northeast lay glacial Lake Ojibwa-Barlow impounded between the height of land on the south and the front of the glacial ice on the north.

In the beginning of this period spruce and pine trees dominated the forests, but by the end of the period pine had won over spruce in the southern parts of the region. At the end of the period there was an increase of spruce in the northern parts of the region following a minor glacial advance, the Cochran, in northern Ontario.

The mastodons probably were gone by this time. Perhaps they had died out or perhaps they had moved northward with the spruce-fir forest, as it followed the retreat of the ice. But deer, elk, and barren-ground caribou were among the animals still inhabiting the region.

The Aqua-Plano Indians made their living by hunting and fishing. In the summertime they lived along the shores and on the islands of glacial and postglacial lakes. Their occupancy of small islands which could not have supported them in the winter months is not only indicative of summer residence but also of the use of boats of some kind.

These ancient Indians operated quarries of quartzite and perhaps taconite. However, their attempts to produce blades with parallel-flaking from such ill-suited stone materials as taconite and quartzite suggest that these Indians had come from or were influenced from areas in which there were flints more suitable for a parallel-flaking technique.

Some dim religious light is cast upon this period by the burial at the Browns Valley site. The presence of weapons, tools, and ornaments placed with the dead is evidence of belief and ritual concerned with supernatural life after death.

Finally, the fact that Aqua-Plano cultural remains have been found much farther north in the Upper Great Lakes region than have been the fluted points of mastodon-hunters suggests, not only that the Aqua-Plano people were later occupants of the region, but also that there was a northward movement of people following the retreating glacier and northward moving zones of vegetation and animals.

The Aqua-Plano tradition gradually disappeared. The Indians either moved northward or their culture shifted to the Boreal Archaic pattern that achieved dominance of the region at a later time.

The Early Archaic culture may have been a part of the Aqua-Plano tradition in the Upper Great Lakes region. More information is needed to settle this point. At the present writing, however, it seems likely that Early Archaic culture overlapped in time with Aqua-Plano culture and if the two were separate entities, then there were Early Archaic Indians in the region at the same time as the Aqua-Plano Indians.

Very little is known about Early Archaic culture in the Upper Great Lakes region. What information is available comes from surface finds within the region and from a few excavated sites in adjacent regions.

The Early Archaic Indians used stemmed and notched spearpoints and knives made of chipped flint, quartzite, and argillite. Their livelihood depended upon hunting and fishing.

The Aqua-Plano and Early Archaic Indians were succeeded in the region by the Boreal Archaic Indians and the Old Copper Indians.

REFERENCES ELSON, 1957; GREENMAN, 1943, 1948, 1953, 1955; GREENMAN and STANLEY, 1943; GRIFFIN, 1956; JENKS, 1937; LEE, 1953, 1954, 1955, 1956, 1957; MacNEISH, 1952; STANLEY, 1941, 1943, 1948, 1953; WORMINGTON, 1957.

6. BOREAL ARCHAIC CULTURE

FROM 5000 TO 500 B.C.

The Indians who left the archeological remains known as the Boreal Archaic culture lived in the Upper Great Lakes region from about 5000 B.C., or earlier, to around 500 B.C. Living in the region at approximately the same time were the Indians identified with the Old Copper culture. These Indians made extensive use of copper in the manufacture of their weapons and tools, whereas most Boreal Archaic groups used little or no copper. Both cultures were forest-adapted and possessed new kinds of woodworking tools that had been lacking in earlier cultures.

These woodworking tools were the ax, the adz, and the gouge (Fig. 17). Boreal Archaic Indians usually made them of fine-grained igneous stone by means of a technique that was also new in this period. Instead of being flaked and chipped, as was done in working flint, the suitably hard stone was pounded or pecked into shape, then smoothed by grinding with other stones, and finally polished. The result was a well-made tool with a hard and sharp cutting edge.

Grooved axes seem to have been the most popular of the stone woodworking tools in the Upper Great Lakes region. Gouges, adzes, and ungrooved axes were relatively rare. There were various sizes and styles of grooved axes, suggesting local specialization within the region. The fluted axes of Wisconsin and the barbed axes of Michigan seem to have been unusual variations originating within this period. Axes were hafted to wooden handles and when used with the proper control and muscular habits were efficient cutting tools. Some modern experiments with stone axes suggest that they work best with short, quick strokes.

This archaic assemblage of woodworking tools was confined to the pine and hardwood (deciduous) forest zones. The pine forests were dominant in the Upper Great Lakes region after 6000 B.C. and the hardwoods were expanding actively by about 4500 B.C. After 3000 B.C. the hardwood forests achieved their maximum northward extension. But regardless of the particular

Fig. 17.—Grooved ax, gouge, and adze of stone Boreal Archaic culture

forest climax at a given time and place, it seems probable that both pine and oaks were available in varying quantity throughout most of the Upper Great Lakes region during the period from 5000 to 500 B.C.

The woodworking tools of these ancient boreal Indians probably were used in the manufacture of various kinds of utensils and the construction of dwellings and dugout canoes. The ax, the gouge, and the adz would be particularly useful in the construction of dugout canoes—craft made by hollowing and shaping a log of suitable size.

The Indian bearers of this early boreal culture lived in various parts of the Upper Great Lakes region from about 5000 to about 500 B.C. They made their living by hunting and fishing and food-collecting. Deer, elk, moose, caribou, and bear were among the animals available to them. They hunted with thrusting spears and with lighter darts or spears hurled with the aid of a spear-thrower (Fig. 18).

The spears were tipped with stemmed or notched points chipped of flint, quartzite, or argillite and sometimes stemmed points of ground and polished slate (Fig. 19).

The spear-thrower probably was a wooden rod or shaft with a hook at its

Fig. 18.—Boreal Archaic Indians hunting moose with spear and spear-thrower

farther end and some kind of grip or handle at its near end. It was equipped with a ground-stone weight (Fig. 20) called a bannerstone that had a central hole through which the rod or shaft was inserted.

In casting the dart or spear, the butt of the shaft was engaged by the hook or projection at the farther end of the spear-thrower while the near end of the spear-thrower was grasped in the hand.

The function of the spear-thrower was to hurl a dart or spear with greater force than could be done by arm and hand alone. It did this by extending the length of the forearm, thus increasing the length of the arc of propulsion of the spear.

Fishing must have been an important part of the economy of these Indians. Fishing equipment included bone fishhooks, gorges of bone or occasionally of copper, notched pebble net-sinkers, nets, probably weirs and traps, and tanged harpoons with multiple barbs on one side. Such harpoon points usually were made of bone, but occasionally were of copper.

Dwellings probably were made of saplings arranged as a frame over which were placed sheets of bark, skins, or mats. Such shelters would be in accord with the necessities of the seminomadic life of archaic woodland hunters.

45

Fig. 19.—Some types of Boreal Archaic blades and spearpoints made of chipped flint, quartzite, and argillite.

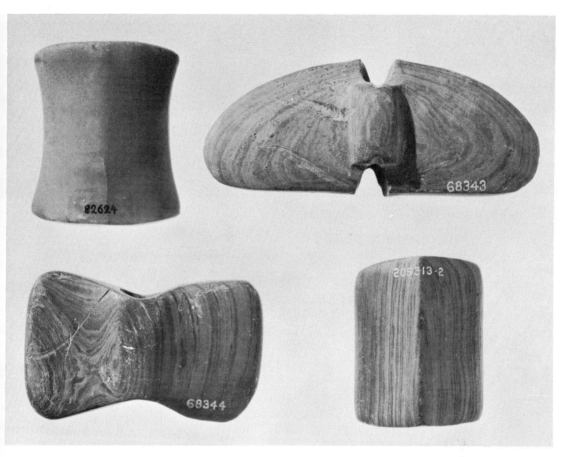

Fig. 20.—Some types of bannerstones

Pottery was lacking. Containers used in cooking probably were of bark or skin, and their liquid contents were heated by the addition of hot rocks, although it is possible to boil water in a birchbark container over an open fire.

Various kinds of scrapers were made of chipped flint. Flaking tools were made of antler, and awls were made of bone or copper. Leaf-shaped knives, stemmed knives, and notched knives were made of chipped flint, quartzite, and argillite. Stemmed knives were occasionally made of ground and polished slate.

The social organization of these Indians must have been relatively simple. Probably small bands of Indians united by ties of kinship utilized large territories for hunting and fishing.

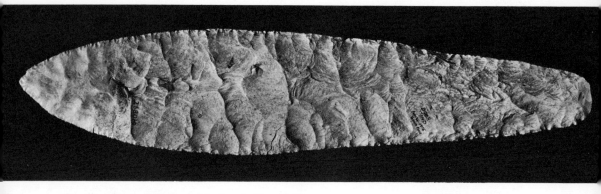

Fig. 21.—*Large leaf-shaped knife of chipped flint*

Fig. 22.—*"Turkey tail" blades of chipped flint*

The deceased were buried, usually in a flexed position, in pits and were accompanied by small amounts of grave goods. Sometimes powdered red ocher was placed in the grave.

For some unknown reason the Boreal Archaic culture achieved a kind of peak or climax from about 1500 to 500 B.C. This seems to have coincided with an increased differentiation of local groupings and is manifested by the addition of some relatively spectacular traits to the existing assemblage.

Among these new traits were leaf-shaped blades of copper almost identical in form to particular leaf-shaped blades of chipped flint; very large leaf-shaped blades of chipped flint (Fig. 21); "turkey tail" knives or spearpoints of dark blue-gray flint (Fig. 22); buried caches of "turkey tail" blades covered with powdered red ocher; buried caches of varieties of leaf-shaped blades also covered with powdered red ocher; copper celts, or axes, that were long and relatively narrow; large copper beads; bar amulets of polished stone, shell gorgets or breast ornaments shaped like the sole of a moccasin, birdstones (Fig. 23), and the liberal use of powdered red ocher in graves and caches.

Most, if not all, of these innovations have been found in association with burials. There is in such burials the implication of more elaborate ceremony in connection with funeral rites and the possibility of special treatment for deceased persons of rank or other distinction. These cultural additions suggest the appearance of a new religious concept or the spread of a burial cult within the region.

These new traits also persist into the subsequent cultural period, when, with certain additions, particularly pottery, they become a part of the Early Woodland culture of the Upper Great Lakes region, an outgrowth of the ancient boreal culture.

The ancient boreal culture that lasted in the Upper Great Lakes region from about 5000 to 500 B.C. is a part of the more generalized boreal culture found not only throughout northeastern North America but also in the northern forest zones of Asia and Europe. There seem to be basic similarities and probably historic connections among all of the boreal groups of the northern hemisphere, but specific details are yet to be demonstrated satisfactorily.

At the present time it appears likely that the ancient boreal culture in the Upper Great Lakes region was the product of migrations from a similar habitat in the northern forest zones of Asia. The Indian carriers of this culture could not have entered the Upper Great Lakes region directly from the north

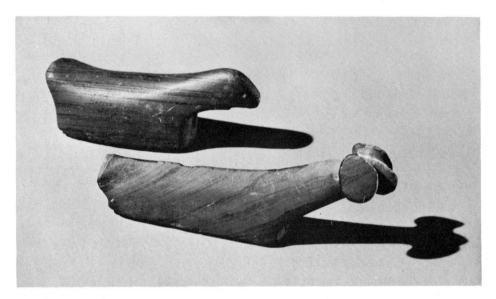

Fig. 23.—Birdstones from northwestern Indiana

because the way was blocked by glacial lakes and lobes of glacial ice west of Hudson's Bay.

The most direct route for Indian migrants coming from the northwest would have been along the western shores of glacial Lake Agassiz to its southern tip and then eastward into the Upper Great Lakes region. It is likely, however, that the earliest Boreal Archaic Indians first established themselves in adjacent areas southwest, south, and southeast of the Upper Great Lakes and subsequently moved into the region.

The Boreal Archaic peoples were contemporaries of the Old Copper Indians in the Upper Great Lakes region, but appear to have antedated them outside of the region. It is entirely possible that the Old Copper Indians were early offshoots of the ancient boreal peoples.

If the Old Copper culture was a derivative of ancient boreal culture, it probably developed independently in the Upper Great Lakes region in fairly close proximity to the sources of raw copper. And copper-working would have evolved independently not as true metallurgy but as the working of a special kind of stone by means of the pecking and grinding technique introduced into North America by the ancient boreal Indians.

The technique of shaping hard igneous stone by pounding and grinding is essentially similar to the shaping of copper by hammering and grinding. Raw copper might have been considered a shining yellow stone with special desirable qualities that made it easy to work into tools and weapons. But with the discovery of annealing—the heating of beaten copper to reduce its brittleness—the Old Copper Indians had gone far beyond mere pounding and grinding. They had taken a step in the direction of metallurgy.

Thus it is possible that the Old Copper culture was a derivative of some earlier stage of ancient boreal culture. But in the Upper Great Lakes region both Old Copper and ancient boreal cultures seem to have been contemporaneous.

In the Upper Great Lakes region both Old Copper and ancient boreal culture carriers occupied different parts of essentially the same habitat. Although future studies may reveal significant differences in adaptation to particular habitats, in general the ancient boreal peoples were subjected to the same environmental changes as the Old Copper Indians. Since these environmental changes will be described in connection with the culture of the Old Copper Indians they will not be given here.

REFERENCES BYERS, 1959; CUNNINGHAM, 1948; GJESSING, 1948; QUIMBY, 1958b; SPAULDING, 1946.

The Old Copper Indians were the first fabricators of metal in the Americas and perhaps in the whole world. Some of them lived as early as six or seven thousand years ago and others survived as late as three thousand years ago.

The known world of the Old Copper Indians was the Upper Great Lakes region. This region underwent radical changes in climate, flora, fauna, and land surface during the periods of Old Copper occupancy. For instance, the lake levels rose as much as 400 feet, the land in places was uplifted nearly 500 feet, and the forest cover changed from pines to hardwoods as the climate became hot. There may even have been a few stray whales in the Lake Huron basin.

The Old Copper Indians were miners and fabricators of copper. All of their copper was mined in the Lake Superior basin, mostly in the upper peninsula of Michigan. There were many mines along the Ontario shore of Lake Superior and there were thousands of prehistoric mining pits on the Keweenaw Peninsula and Isle Royale in Upper Michigan.

Remnants of wooden levers, fragmentary birchbark buckets, hammerstones, and charcoal from fires have been found in old mining pits, some of which were at least twenty feet deep. From such archeological evidence the techniques of prehistoric copper mining have been reconstructed.

The method of mining was as follows. The Indian miners followed the veins of pure copper from surface outcrops by digging pits and breaking the copper from its rock matrix with the aid of fire and water and large beach boulders used as hammers. The rock surrounding the pure copper was heated by fire, then cracked by sudden chilling with cold water, then pounded loose with boulder hammers and pried away with wooden levers. The copper thus obtained was transported to camps and villages where it was fashioned into tools, weapons, and ornaments.

Smelting and casting of copper were unknown. The pure copper was shaped

Fig. 24.—Socketed spearpoints of copper—Old Copper culture

into the intended form by cold-hammering and annealing—pounding the copper and heating and chilling it to keep it from becoming too brittle.

Most of the copper was fashioned into tools and weapons. Among the copper weapons were various types of socketed spearpoints (Fig. 24) and knives; various types of spearpoints lacking sockets but possessing different kinds of tangs (Figs. 25, 26); some varieties of leaf-shaped knives and spearpoints; conical spearpoints; and socketed pikes that were long, narrow instruments, rectangular in section with sharp points.

There were also copper fishhooks, gorges, and socketed harpoon points with single barbs.

Copper tools included socketed axes or adzes (Fig. 27), also called spuds, that were hafted to handles made of wood or of elk or caribou antler; various kinds of knives with straight or curved blades and sockets or tangs for fasten-

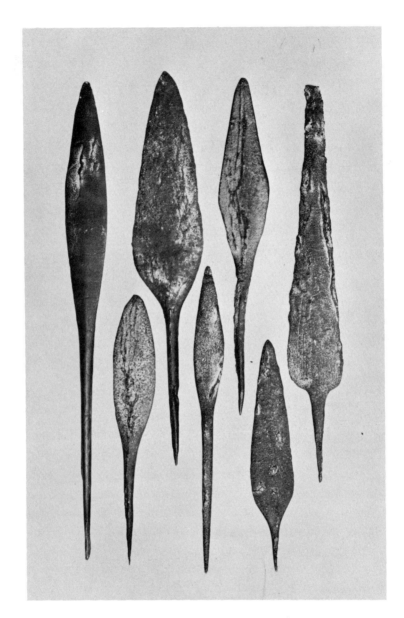

Fig. 25.—Copper spearpoints with tangs—Old Copper culture

Fig. 26.—Tools and weapon points of copper. UPPER LEFT *is chisel;* UPPER RIGHT *is spearpoint with flat tang;* LOWER LEFT *is crescent-shaped knife; and* LOWER RIGHT *is spearpoint with flat tang.*

ing to handles (Fig. 28); and crescent-shaped knives like Eskimo ulos, some of which had two prongs for attachment to handles of bone or wood (Fig. 26).

Some additional tools were gouges (Fig. 27), chisels (Fig. 26), awls, wedges, punches, needles, pikes, drills, celts, and spatulate forms of unknown use.

Copper ornaments were rare. Among those ornaments were thin tubular beads; thick spheroidal beads; thick C-shaped bracelets, some with incised zigzag designs; thin C-shaped bracelets with ornamental bosses; thin pendants, rectangular, round, or ovate, and thin copper strips that were used like inverted pendants as part of a crown-shaped headdress.

In addition to those of copper, there have been found tools and weapons of stone and bone and ornaments of shell. These include side-notched knives and projectile points of chipped flint, various types of scraping and cutting tools of chipped flint; mauls made of beach cobbles; hammerstones; antler flaking-tools, and handles made of antler. Whistles and other tubular objects were made of bird bone, and beads of several styles were made of imported marine shells and the shells of pond snails.

Birchbark was used for the manufacture of containers and probably many other things, including possibly canoes.

Fig. 27.—Socketed axes and gouge of copper—Old Copper culture

The Old Copper Indians, as indicated by a limited sample of their skeletal remains, were rather tall, fairly robust, and well developed muscularly. They had long heads, moderately high vaults with some saggital cresting, and relatively narrow faces.

The Old Copper Indians made their living by hunting and fishing. Among the animals they hunted were deer, elk, barren-ground caribou, lynx, and probably bison. Ducks, swans, cranes, and owls were among the birds taken. These Indians hunted with the spear and probably the spear-thrower. Fish were taken with nets, spears, harpoons, hooks, and gorges.

The Old Copper people seem to have been the first in the Upper Great Lakes region to have dogs. There were two kinds: a small dog about the size of a coyote and a large one about the size of the largest known Eskimo dogs.

Boats of some kind certainly were used by the Old Copper Indians. Their use of island areas that could not have supported any winter population demanded the use of boats. Probably these craft were wooden dugouts, canoes

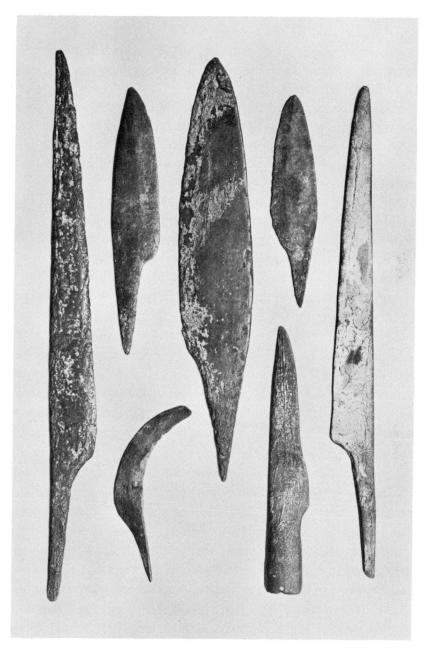

Fig. 28.—Some copper knives of the Old Copper culture

made by hollowing and shaping suitable logs, but it is possible that the birch-bark canoe also existed by this time.

Although no definitely identified dwellings have been found, at one site in northern Wisconsin there were post holes suggesting an oval structure about 13 feet in diameter.

The dead were buried in cemeteries. The Old Copper grave pits contained multiple and single interments in a variety of positions. There were extended and flexed primary burials, secondary burials of bones in bundles, and cre-mations. With the dead were placed tools, weapons, and ornaments for use in the spirit world.

The locations of some Old Copper sites are indicated on the map (Fig. 29).

The Old Copper culture is an ancient one in the Upper Great Lakes region. Some measure of its antiquity is provided by radiocarbon dates as early as 5556 and 3646 B.C. and others of 1845, 1702, and 1492 B.C. Occasional copper arti-facts representative of the Old Copper culture have been found in New York, Illinois, and Kentucky with Archaic cultural remains radiocarbon-dated at about 3000 B.C. or earlier.

In addition there is good geological evidence in support of an early date for the beginnings of the Old Copper culture. For instance, the locations of a number of finds of Old Copper artifacts as well as some Old Copper sites are in areas that would have been under water during the Lake Algonquin stage and the Nipissing stage of the Upper Great Lakes. There are at least three places where evidence indicates that Old Copper materials were covered by deposits and water planes of the Nipissing stage. Therefore these particular sites and finds must have been in position after the Algonquin stage and prior to the Nipissing stage. Since the Nipissing stage is shown by radiocarbon dating to have been as early as about 3000 B.C., it would seem that these par-ticular Old Copper sites and finds must belong to a period prior to that time. Hence the geological evidence shows that some Old Copper sites and finds are pre-Nipissing in age and therefore older than 3000 B.C., thus confirming the assessment of age based upon the radiocarbon dates from an actual Old Copper site. It seems clear then that the Old Copper culture had its begin-nings in very ancient times, most likely by at least 5000 B.C. However, the Old Copper culture lasted for many centuries, probably until the end of the Nipissing stage of the Upper Great Lakes, about 1500 B.C.

The environment of the Upper Great Lakes, the world known to the Old

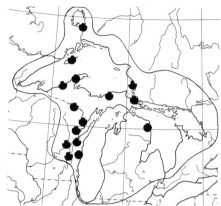

Fig. 29.—Map showing distribution of Old Copper sites and copper mines in Upper Great Lakes region.

Copper Indians, was certainly different from ours, particularly in the Chippewa-Stanley stage of the lakes lasting until about 3000 B.C., or slightly later.

First of all, the lake levels were hundreds of feet lower than today. In the Lake Michigan basin, Lake Chippewa was 350 feet below the present lake level. In the Lake Huron basin, Lake Stanley was 400 feet beneath the present lake level. And the waters in the Lake Superior basin were some hundreds of feet lower (see Fig. 8, chap. iii).

During this period there were two additional large lakes in the region. To the northwest lay glacial Lake Agassiz, which at this time drained eastward to the Superior basin, and on the northeast were the remnants of glacial Lake Ojibwa-Barlow, which at its maximum was a tremendous body of water caught between the ice front and the height of land. This glacial lake was drained to near extinction sometime during the Chippewa-Stanley stage, so it is likely that only the earliest Old Copper Indians would have had it on the northern periphery of their environment. Lake Agassiz, on the other hand, seems to have persisted much longer, lasting at least into the time of the Nipissing stage. Artifacts representative of the Old Copper culture have been found on old beaches of glacial Lake Agassiz in Minnesota and Canada, suggesting that some Old Copper Indians actually lived on the shores of Lake Agassiz.

Lake Chippewa drained into Lake Stanley by means of a long river through what is now Mackinac Straits. Lake Stanley drained to the Atlantic Ocean by way of the Ottawa River through the North Bay, Ontario, outlet which at that time stood nearly at sea level (see Fig. 8, chap. iii).

With such drastically lowered lake levels, there was of course an appreciable difference in the relation of water and land. What is now the present lake shore would have been 25 miles or more inland in many places, whereas the former lake shore now lies under 350 or 400 feet of water.

In the northwestern part of the Lake Michigan basin near Green Bay, there would have been limestone hills down which ran rivers with tremendous rapids or perhaps waterfalls which dropped 200 or 300 feet. A similar situation would have existed in much of the Superior basin and along the northern and eastern shores of Lake Stanley in the Huron basin.

Along much of the western shore of Lake Chippewa were sloping clay hills covered with deciduous forest. Remnants of this forest can still be found far beneath the waters of Lake Michigan just off Racine, Wisconsin. But at the time this forest flourished one could have walked directly from Racine to Michigan City, Indiana, or from Chicago to Benton Harbor, Michigan, through woods and dune areas on trails that today could only be followed by fish or submarines.

Along the east shore of Lake Chippewa there were sand hills, sloping sand plains, and rivers where now there is the deep water of Lake Michigan.

The area embraced by the city of Chicago would have been 360 to 370 feet above the level of Lake Chippewa and 30 miles southwest of its nearest shore.

From these examples one can see that the topography was much different from that of modern times. The climate, flora, and fauna were different too.

About 6000 B.C., at the beginning of the Chippewa-Stanley stage, the ice front was in northern Ontario at about the latitude of the city of Cochrane. By the middle of the period the ice had retreated northward from this position. (See Fig. 8, chap. iii.) The climate was becoming increasingly warmer during the Lake Chippewa–Stanley stage and was actually hot by the end of the stage, *circa* 3000 B.C.

By the time of the beginnings of the Old Copper culture the spruce-fir forest had already retreated northward and pine had achieved a dominance of the forests over much of the region. With the dominance of pine had come an increase in the expansion of grasses, particularly in the western parts of the Old Copper world.

During the early stages of the Old Copper culture in the last half of the Lake Chippewa–Stanley period the pine dominance began to give way to the expansion of the hardwood forests with their oak and chestnut, and the grasslands encroached even more upon the forests.

The Chippewa-Stanley stage was terminated by the upwarping of the land in the vicinity of the North Bay outlet by more than 400 feet, presumably caused by the postglacial expansion of the earth released from the weight of the glacial ice, which had retreated from the area some thousands of years earlier. With the North Bay outlet thus closed, there was a tremendous rise in water levels, climaxed by the Nipissing stage of the Upper Great Lakes, which lasted from shortly after 3000 to about 1500 B.C. Instead of a single outlet at North Bay there were two outlets, one at Chicago and another at Port Huron. (See Fig. 9, chap. iii.)

The amount of rise in the Superior basin is not known, but it must have been considerable. The water in the Lake Michigan basin rose 375 feet and the level in the Huron basin rose at least 425 feet to a single body of water with a plane about 25 feet above the present level in these basins.

The shoreline sites of the Old Copper Indians who had lived during the second half of the Chippewa-Stanley stage were covered by hundreds of feet of water and are still covered in the southern parts of the Upper Great Lakes region where there has been no appreciable upwarping.

During the Nipissing stage the climate was much hotter than at present or any other time during the last 18,000 or more years. Forests dominated by oak and hickory reached their maximum northward extension and the pine and spruce stands were pushed even farther northward too. This was the time of the greatest extent of grasslands in eastern North America.

Among the animals living in the Upper Great Lakes region in the days when Old Copper Indians lived in the area were deer, elk, barren-ground caribou, lynx, beaver, and bison. There is some evidence of whales in the Huron basin, inasmuch as whale remains have been found in a Nipissing-stage beach deposit. Occasional whales may well have entered the Huron basin from the Atlantic by way of the North Bay outlet during the Chippewa-Stanley low-water stage. Although whales were not economically important to the Indians, they may well have been incorporated into religious beliefs as sea monsters.

The Old Copper culture, as such, disappeared from the Upper Great Lakes region about 1500 B.C., or perhaps somewhat later. One of the factors in the disappearance of the Old Copper culture must have been the northward movement of the boreal forest following the retreat of the glacial ice.

Northernmost Old Copper sites in the Upper Great Lakes region are more recent than the southern ones. There are, for instance, finds of Old Copper artifacts on the bed of glacial Lake Agassiz in Manitoba. Such artifacts must postdate glacial Lake Agassiz and are much later than artifacts from the earliest sites in Wisconsin. Moreover, the bed of glacial Lake Agassiz was not available for occupancy during the earlier stages of Old Copper culture. There is thus some evidence indicating that the Old Copper culture is latest in the northern part of the region.

It seems reasonable to believe that, as their accustomed type of forests and animals began to retreat northward after 3000 B.C., some of the Old Copper Indians moved northward too. Their old homeland must have presented many problems in terms of changing climate, water levels, available land areas, and topography. Moreover, like other primitive cultures based on a hunting economy, the Old Copper culture must have been closely tied to its environment through the interaction of habitat and culture. Thus as their ecological zone moved northward so did some of the Old Copper Indians.

The northward trail of the Old Copper Indians disappears in Manitoba directly on the line of march between Lake Superior and Coronation Gulf. How late the Old Copper culture may have persisted in this area is not now known. But in A.D. 1771, Samuel Hearne reported copper artifacts among the Indians and Eskimos between Churchill and the mouth of the Coppermine River.

Hearne mentioned bayonet-like blades, knives, adzes, crescent-shaped knives, ice chisels, awls, and arrowheads of copper made by cold-hammering and annealing. This copper industry might well represent the last vestige of the Old Copper culture surviving in a peripheral region into the period of written history.

Those Old Copper Indians who did not move northward found themselves in a new environment because of the change in climate. Their culture probably changed in response to the new environment and perhaps some of them were assimilated by other Boreal Archaic Indians who had occupied other parts of the Upper Great Lakes region since about 5000 B.C. Possibly the Old Copper culture is, in part, ancestral to and responsible for the climax in the late Boreal Archaic culture that appeared in the region after 1500 B.C.

In any event, the manufacture of many typical Old Copper styles of tools and weapons disappeared in the Upper Great Lakes region. However, the technique of working copper by cold-hammering and annealing persisted into subsequent periods. For instance, specific forms of copper tools and weapons were made in limited quantities by some of the groups of Indians dwelling in the region from about 1500 to 200 B.C. And in 100 B.C. there was a renaissance of copper-working, when the Hopewell Indians began their extensive manufacture of ornaments and ceremonial objects.

REFERENCES BAERREIS, DAIFUKU, and LUNSTED, 1954; HEARNE, 1795; POPHAM and EMERSON, 1954; QUIMBY, 1954, 1957, fieldnotes; QUIMBY and SPAULDING, 1957; RITZENTHALER, 1958; RITZENTHALER et al., 1956; RITZENTHALER and WITTRY, 1952; SPAULDING, 1957, 1957a; WITTRY, 1951; WITTRY and RITZENTHALER, 1956.

8. BURIAL MOUNDS AND POTTERY

500 TO 100 B.C.

Burial mounds and/or pottery were the most obvious characteristics of the Early Woodland culture that existed from about 500 to 100 B.C. in parts of the Upper Great Lakes region south of Lake Superior.

In this area the Early Woodland culture was the product of a mixture of late Boreal Archaic characteristics and new traits introduced into the region. The Boreal Archaic ancestry of Early Woodland sprang from the groups of Indians whose culture was part of the peak or climax of this region in the period between 1500 and 500 B.C. The new traits added to this older culture probably entered the region from the south and the east.

The origin of burial mounds is unknown. Possibly they diffused to America from the northern forest zone of Asia. Possibly they developed independently in the glaciated regions in and adjacent to the Upper Great Lakes. If so, they must have had their ancestry in the late Boreal Archaic custom of using raised places such as sand ridges and kames or gravelly knobs for burial of the dead. At the present time, however, it rather looks as if burial mounds were earlier in regions south of the Upper Great Lakes. It is therefore probable that the burial mound complex entered the Upper Great Lakes region from the Ohio or Mississippi valleys and their tributaries.

Burial mounds (Fig. 30) were erected over the graves of the dead. The recently deceased were arranged in a flexed position, and the remains of people that presumably had been placed in trees or on platforms on a temporary basis were wrapped in bundles and laid in the burial place. A few of the dead were cremated. Tools, utensils, weapons, ornaments, and powdered red ocher were put with the corpses either in a shallow grave or upon a prepared surface. Then a dome-shaped mound of earth was built over the grave.

Probably not everyone was buried in a mound. Mound burial may have been accorded only to persons of great prestige in religious or civil affairs. And such burials do indicate a greater expenditure of wealth and energy on death rituals than had been customary in previous periods.

Fig. 30.—Drawing of burial mound

Pottery, the other important new addition to Upper Great Lakes culture of the Early Woodland period, was of two kinds. There was a very thick, grit-tempered ware with exterior surfaces—and sometimes interior surfaces as well—covered with the impressions of fabric, or of a cord-wrapped paddle-like object. Vessels of this ware seem to have been broad-mouthed jars with conoidal bottoms (Fig. 31).

There was also a thinner, grit-tempered ware, frequently plain, sometimes cord-marked, and often decorated with stamped or punctate designs (Fig. 31). The stamped designs were composed of elements made with a simple dentate stamp, a rocked dentate stamp, or a serpentine stamp resembling the edge of a scallop shell. The designs were applied to the body and rim areas of wide-mouthed jars that had straight vertical rims or slightly flaring rims and conoidal bottoms.

These Early Woodland ceramic wares were part of a pottery tradition found throughout the northern forest zones of Europe and Asia. It is probable that such pottery diffused from the northern forest zone of Siberia to the northern forest zone of America and eventually reached the eastern seaboard. These pottery styles seem to have undergone development in centers south or east of the Upper Great Lakes before they entered the region. Such pottery

Fig. 31.—Early Woodland pottery

in fact appears to be older in the East than it is in the Upper Great Lakes region, a puzzling situation that may be cleared up by future research.

The Early Woodland Indians made their living by hunting, fishing, and the gathering of wild foods and materials present in their habitat. They had no domestic animals except dogs.

They hunted the deer, elk, moose, beaver, and other animals. They used spears, probably of several kinds, including those cast with a spear-thrower and they may have had the bow and arrow. Projectile points were stemmed or notched varieties made of chipped flint or quartzite (Fig. 32). There were several kinds of large spearpoints. These included the "turkey tail" blades of blue gray flint, various stemmed points of flint and quartzite, and probably occasional forms of ground slate.

Fish were taken with spears, nets, and probably hooks and traps. Nets were weighted with notched sinkers made of flat beach cobbles. Fish spears were tipped with unilaterally barbed harpoon-like points of bone or copper. Fishhooks were probably made of bone. Among the fish taken were sturgeon, mullet, sucker, and pickerel.

There is no direct evidence of dwelling type available, but probably the Indians of the Early Woodland period lived in wigwams made of a pole framework covered with skins, bark, or mats.

Household utensils included pottery vessels and in all likelihood containers made of bark, wood, or shell. Iron pyrites and probably wooden friction drills were employed in making fire.

Tools included ungrooved axes of stone or copper (Fig. 33); crude celtlike

Fig. 32.—Early Woodland points of chipped flint

Fig. 33.—Copper awl and copper axes

blades of chipped sedimentary stone; large leaf-shaped knives of chipped flint; awls of bone or copper (Fig. 33); roughly flaked core scrapers of flint and quartzite; flint flakes used as knives and scrapers; truncated leaf-shaped blades of chipped flint, often lopsided; and end scrapers of chipped flint and quartzite.

Among the ornaments used by Upper Great Lakes Indians of the Early Woodland period were large spheroidal beads of copper (Fig. 34); gorgets, or breast ornaments, of ground and polished slate; tubular beads of rolled sheet copper; bar amulets of ground and polished stone (Fig. 35); pear-shaped and circular gorgets of imported marine shell; and birdstones usually of ground and polished slate.

The function of birdstones is unknown and they may not have been orna-ments. Basal perforations suggest they once were fastened to something and it is possible that birdstones were used as weights on spear-thrower shafts or

Fig. 34.—Necklace of thick copper beads

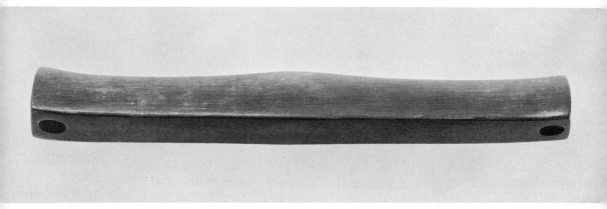

Fig. 35.—Bar amulet of ground and polished slate

served some other equally utilitarian purpose, such as ornamental handles for spear-throwers.

Ceremonial life of the Early Woodland Indians was manifested in their use of burial mounds and in the quality and quantity of tools, weapons, ornaments, and utensils placed in graves and often sprinkled liberally with powdered red ocher. It is possible that the large leaf-shaped blades found in graves were especially made for burial with the dead.

Still another manifestation of ceremonial life may have been the buried caches of truncated, asymmetric, leaf-shaped blades that also frequently were colored with powdered red ocher.

It is also possible that smoking of tobacco or some other leaf was a ceremonial activity of some Early Woodland Indians. Stone tubes similar to those identified as smoking pipes in adjacent regions have been found in at least one of the excavated Early Woodland sites of the Upper Great Lakes region. Moreover, occasional surface finds of tubular pipes have been made in the region. But tubular pipes are rare in the Upper Great Lakes and probably are an expression of the introduction of smoking from other regions lying south or east.

Although most of the archeological remains indicative of Early Woodland culture in the Upper Great Lakes region consist of surface finds, there are data from some five or more excavated sites in Wisconsin, Michigan, and Ontario.

These sites were located in the Lake Nipissing basin and Mattawa Valley areas, the Lake Huron basin in Ontario and Michigan, and the Lake Michigan basin in Michigan, Indiana, and Wisconsin.

Some of these sites are in locations lower than the Algoma stage beach and on the lakeward side of the beach. This situation means that these sites must be younger than the Algoma stage beach which dates at about 1500 B.C. and later. Fortunately, there are radiocarbon datings available from three of the sites in the Lake Huron and Lake Nipissing basins.

At the Frank Bay site, Lake Nipissing, the Early Woodland materials are above and later than the Boreal Archaic cultural stratum dated at 965 B.C. An Early Woodland site associated with a post-Algoma beach near Killarney, Ontario, in the northern end of the Lake Huron basin has been dated at 225 B.C. The Burley site in the southeastern Lake Huron basin has a date of 667 B.C. These radiocarbon datings are compatible with the estimate of about 500 to 100 B.C. for the duration of the Early Woodland period in the Upper Great Lakes region.

REFERENCES   CRANE, 1956; CUNNINGHAM, 1948; FOX, 1930;
GREENMAN, 1948, 1951, 1953;
GREENMAN and STANLEY, 1940, 1941;
GRIFFIN, personal communication; JURY, 1952;
MASON, personal communication; QUIMBY, 1958a;
RIDLEY, 1954.

9. THE HOPEWELL INDIANS AND THE
BEGINNINGS OF AGRICULTURE
IN THE REGION

The Hopewell Indians were a prehistoric mound-building people who occupied parts of the eastern United States for more than a thousand years beginning around 500 B.C. Their primary cultural centers were in the central Mississippi, Ohio, and Illinois river valleys. These Indians were farmers, traders, and artists of exceptional ability.

About 100 B.C. some groups of Hopewell Indians entered the Upper Great Lakes region from their cultural center in the Illinois River Valley. Being a riverine people, they traveled up the Illinois River to the Kankakee, then they followed the Kankakee River to its headwaters in northwestern Indiana and crossed the portage to the St. Joseph River Valley of southwestern Michigan.

After establishing their settlements and ceremonial centers along the upper Kankakee and lower St. Joseph rivers, the Hopewell Indians went northward in western Michigan, probably first to the Kalamazoo Valley, then to the lower Grand River Valley where they established an important ceremonial center at the present site of Grand Rapids.

Somewhat later, groups of Grand River Hopewellians settled in the valley of the Muskegon River. This was the northernmost occupancy of the Upper Great Lakes region by Hopewell Indians, although in the Upper Mississippi region of western Wisconsin other groups of Hopewell Indians had settled even farther north.

In either case the northernmost occupancy of each region by Hopewell Indians was within a deciduous forest zone which at that time probably was dominated by oak and hickory, but which in historic times was composed principally of maple, beech, birch, and hemlock.

The northernmost occupancy of Hopewell Indians in both the Upper Great Lakes and Upper Mississippi regions was also limited by climate. They favored a relatively warm climate and did not settle north of the line that in modern times designates a frost-free season of at least 150 days. (The southern boundary of Köppen's Dfb type of climate also marks the northern limit of the Hopewell territory.)

This climatic limitation on the Hopewell Indians must have been related to their agricultural pursuits. They made their living by farming and supplemented their food production by hunting and fishing. They raised corn, squash, perhaps beans, and probably tobacco. But corn-growing most likely was limited by the climate. It seems probable that in Hopewell times, the tropical flint corn had not yet been adapted to growth in cooler regions. Yet by A.D. 1700 a hardier Indian corn was being raised on the south side of Lake Superior, well north of the zone of Hopewell occupancy and in an era of cooler world climate. But the Hopewell Indians seem to have been the first farmers in the region, and their habitat was limited to the areas where the somewhat delicate tropical flint corn of that period could be grown.

The Hopewell Indians seem to have hunted all of the available animals, particularly deer. These animals included all or nearly all of those still found in the region when the first Europeans arrived nearly 1,000 years after the end of Hopewell culture. The only domesticated animal of the Hopewell Indians was the dog.

The physical appearance of the Hopewell Indians can be reconstructed from their skeletons and some small sculptured figures found in their burial places. These Indians were of medium height and longheaded or medium longheaded. The figurines suggest that they were stocky or plump, particularly the women, with oval faces and "slant" eyes.

The men wore breech cloths of animal skin or woven fabric and the women wore wrap-around skirts of woven cloth or skin. Both men and women wore slipper-like moccasins, probably made of animal skin.

Women seem to have worn their hair long in back but parted in the middle on top of the head and drawn back above the ears. Men removed some of their hair leaving a forelock in front and long hair gathered into a knot at the back of the head.

Their dwellings probably were types of wigwams, round or oval in plan with dome-shaped roofs, made of saplings covered with bark, mats, or skins.

Their villages and ceremonial centers were always along rivers. They erected large conical or dome-shaped mounds of earth over the dead (Fig. 36) and built earthen walls inclosing large areas that were circular, oval, or rectangular.

Fig. 36.—Reconstruction of partly excavated Hopewell burial mound, showing burials and accompanying grave offerings.

The largest Hopewell ceremonial center in the Upper Great Lakes region was at the present site of Grand Rapids, Michigan. Near the center of the city on the west side of the Grand River there formerly stood a group of about thirty to forty mounds, the largest of which was at least 30 feet high and 200 feet in circumference. On the opposite side of the river, about two miles south of the city, there is a group of fifteen mounds, the largest of which is 15 feet high and about 100 feet in diameter. There once seems to have been associated with this mound group a large rectangular inclosure with low walls of earth.

A Hopewell site in the St. Joseph River Valley at which there was a group of nine mounds was associated with an inclosure about 80 feet wide and 110 feet long, shaped like a horseshoe. The walls of earth have disappeared but the outline of the inclosure still shows in aerial photographs. In the Ohio

Hopewell center there are many very elaborate earth wall inclosures constructed by the Indians.

During a part of each summer, some groups of Hopewell Indians left their settlements on the rivers and moved to the shore of Lake Michigan. These summer campsites were always located in sheltered hollows among sand dunes, usually in areas of land between Lake Michigan and an inland lake or river estuary. Food refuse collected from one of these sites included remains of bear, beaver, deer, wolf, muskrat, rabbit, largemouth bass, channel catfish, sheepshead, painted turtle, and mussels.

The Hopewell Indians made great use of exotic raw materials for the manufacture of tools, weapons, ornaments, and objects used in religious ceremonies. To obtain these raw materials they engaged in widespread trade and commerce.

From the Rocky Mountain region of the far West they obtained obsidian for their ceremonial blades and grizzly bear teeth for ornaments. Large marine shells came from the south Atlantic coast and the Gulf of Mexico. Copper and silver came from the mines in the western Lake Superior area, and mica sheets came from the middle Atlantic coastal region. Galena, or lead, was brought into the Upper Great Lakes region from Missouri and northwestern Illinois.

Tools and weapons were made of copper, stone, and bone (Fig. 37). There were ungrooved axes of copper and polished stone; awls of bone, antler, and copper; corner-notched projectile points of chipped flint (Fig. 38); knives of chipped flint and obsidian; needles of bone and copper; small flake knives; large ceremonial blades of chipped flint of unusual coloring; graving tools of stone, beaver incisors, and copper; and scrapers and drills of chipped flint.

The Hopewell Indians had musical instruments. Most characteristic were panpipes consisting of three or four conjoined tubes of bone or reed, graduated in length, and bound together with a broad, flat, encircling band of silver or copper. They also had rattles of various kinds, including some made of turtle shell, and probably they had drums.

Tobacco pipes made of polished stone were of the platform-type with a bowl centered on a platform and a stem hole from one end of the platform to the bowl (Fig. 39). Most such pipes were simple, symmetrical, curved-base platforms with spool or barrel-shaped bowls. Some were elaborate effigy forms with bowls carved realistically in the form of animals and humans.

One such pipe had a bowl carved in the form of a bear, another had a bowl

Fig. 37.—Copper tools and ornaments of the Hopewell Indians. A-C *awls;* D *bead;*
E-H *axes;* I-J *beads;* K-L *axes;* M-N *awls;* O-P *ear ornaments;* Q *needle;* R-W *axes. Note fabric*
impressions on F, G, H, L, V, *and* W.

Fig. 38.—Hopewell type projectile points

in the form of a nude woman seated on the platform, her cradled baby in front of her (Fig. 39). Still another pipe with two bowls had a platform carved to represent an alligator (Fig. 39).

The Hopewell Indians had fine pottery and utensils. There were spoons made of notched mussel shells and probably of wood. Large dippers or containers were made of imported marine shells.

Pottery was of several styles. There was a utilitarian ware consisting of round- or conoidal-based jars made of fired clay tempered with particles of granitic stone and covered on the exterior with the imprints of a cord-wrapped paddle.

A characteristic Hopewellian ware similar in paste and form to the ware just described differed in that the exterior surface was smoothed and then decorated with bands and zones of rather thick dentate stamp impressions.

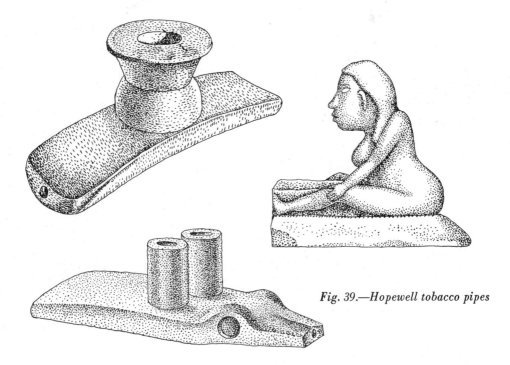

Fig. 39.—Hopewell tobacco pipes

The finest pottery ever found in the prehistoric Upper Great Lakes region was the Hopewell ceremonial ware made of fired clay tempered with small particles of limestone. Characteristic of this type were small quadrilobate jars with flat bottoms. The smooth, gray surfaces of such vessels were decorated with contrasting body zones filled with closely spaced impressions of a fine-toothed dentate stamp rocked back and forth, and the rims were decorated with a band of fine cross-hatching. This pottery probably was made only for burial with the dead.

Some other Hopewell pottery types seem to have been copies of this fine ceremonial ware. These types, represented by jars with round or flat bottoms and bodies that frequently were quadrilobate, were made of fired clay tempered with particles of granitic stone. Some of this pottery was relatively plain, but most of it was decorated with curvilinear zones filled with curved zigzag lines or punctate impressions (Fig. 40).

Ornaments of the Hopewell Indians were made of metal, shell, bone, and stone. Beads for necklaces were made of copper (Fig. 37), river pearls, marine shell, and the canine teeth of bears. Spool-shaped ear ornaments of copper

Fig. 40.—Hopewell pottery from burial mounds in western Michigan

(Fig. 37) were on some occasions worn at the wrists. There were armbands of silver and probably of copper. Pendants and breast ornaments included those of polished stone, copper, perforated and cut animal jaws, bone and copper effigies of animal teeth, perforated eagle claws, and bear canine teeth inlaid with river pearls. Pieces of imported sheet mica may have been used as ornaments or mirrors.

The Hopewell Indians wove cloth by means of finger techniques rather than on a loom. Twining was the most common method of weaving. Thread was twisted by hand from bast fiber—the soft inner bark of certain trees.

The Hopewell Indians were the outstanding artists of the Upper Great Lakes region and their products were never surpassed by the Indians who lived in the region in later times.

The elaborate effigy forms made of sheet copper and mica, the complicated geometric forms in copper made probably from folded patterns, and the delicate engraving on bone, shell, and wood so characteristic of the Ohio Hopewell center were lacking in the Upper Great Lakes region. But the other art forms were present, particularly sculpture in stone and bone portraying humans, animals, birds, fishes, reptiles, and insects. Probably all of Hopewell art had religious and ceremonial significance.

Hopewell art and material wealth were lavished on the dead, probably with elaborate ceremonies. Deceased people of high rank were placed in subfloor pits or tombs sometimes lined with bark or logs. Tools, weapons, utensils, pottery, pipes, and ceremonial objects, all of excellent quality, were placed in the grave. Bodies were placed in an extended or a flexed position. Bundles of bones, probably from partly decomposed bodies that had been placed on burial scaffolds, were also placed in grave pits.

When the burials were completed large mounds of earth were erected over the grave pits. These mounds were conical or dome-shaped. It is likely that only individuals of high social position, such as priests and chiefs or members of ruling families, were given mound burial.

The Hopewell Indians must have had a social organization that included class structures; hereditary ranks and privileges; divisions of labor; ways of organizing co-operative work projects, such as the building of mounds and inclosures; and means for individuals to become specialized as artists, traders, metal workers, and the like. This social organization, whatever its actual details, was much more elaborate than that of any of the earlier prehistoric groups of Indians in the Upper Great Lakes region.

The period of Hopewell culture in this region was from about 100 B.C. to A.D. 700. This dating is derived from cross-ties between the ceramic stratigraphy in the Upper Great Lakes region and that of the Illinois Valley Hopewell center, where there is an adequate number of radiocarbon-dated sites.

Hopewell culture in the Upper Great Lakes region, as well as elsewhere in the eastern United States, represents a climax of culture—a kind of classical period, the like of which was never achieved again.

Hopewell culture was based on agriculture, which was sufficiently developed to permit a stable mode of life. Agriculture originated in tropical America some thousands of years prior to its introduction into the Upper Great Lakes region. From its centers in the nucleus of America, agriculture based on the cultivation of corn, squash, and beans gradually diffused to various parts of North America, but not all of the crops in this tropical assemblage diffused at the same time or to the same places. However, by about 100 B.C., the probable time of its introduction into the Upper Great Lakes region, agriculture was well established elsewhere in North America and most likely squash and

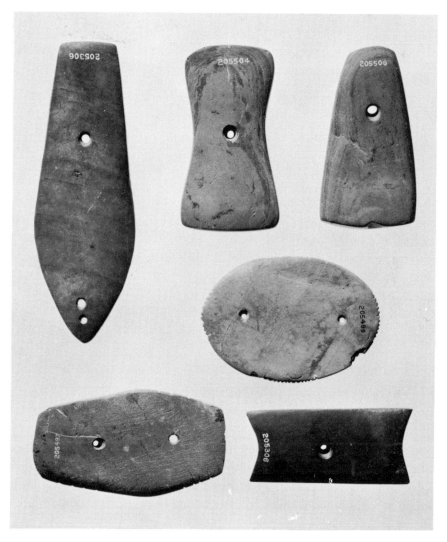

Fig. 41.—Gorgets of ground slate

beans, as well as tropical flint corn, were brought into the Upper Great Lakes region from the Illinois River Valley by migrating Hopewell Indians.

There were other Indians living in the Upper Great Lakes at the same time as the Hopewell Indians. These neighbors of the Hopewell people had a much simpler culture. Some of them made their living by farming and hunting—others only by hunting and fishing.

Fig. 42.—Cord-marked pottery of the Middle Woodland period

They used stemmed and notched arrows and spearpoints of chipped flint, ungrooved axes or celts of ground stone or copper, stemmed and notched knives of chipped flint, awls of bone and copper, chipped flint drills, bone harpoon points with barbs, antler flaking-tools, and various kinds of flint scrapers.

There were beads of shell or small beads of rolled sheet copper and breast ornaments or gorgets of ground slate (Fig. 41).

They had elbow pipes of fired clay and sometimes effigy pipes of clay and stone.

Their pottery consisted of jars with rather straight rims and round or semi-conoidal bottoms (Fig. 42). These were made of clay tempered with particles of granitic stone. Exterior vessel surfaces were frequently covered completely with impressions of a cord-wrapped paddle, but in some eastern areas of the region there was a ware with smooth surfaces and rim and upper body decorations of a simple geometric pattern produced by rather crude stamping with dentate stamps or punching with a pointed tool.

Dwellings probably were circular or oval in ground plan, conical or dome-shaped, made of large saplings, and covered with bark, skins, or woven mats.

The dead, often accompanied by grave offerings, were buried in cemeteries or in subfloor pits beneath small mounds. Bodies were flexed or extended. There were also bundle burials and sometimes cremations.

In addition to burial mounds, some of these neighbors of the Hopewell Indians constructed large circular inclosures—embankments of earth inclosing a circular area. Either they or the Hopewell Indians also seem to have been responsible for the so-called garden beds in southern Michigan.

Garden beds were low earth ridges about 18 inches high arranged in precise geometric forms, somewhat like an old-fashioned formal garden. Most were of rectilinear patterns of varying complexity, but some were shaped like wagon wheels. The largest of these garden beds embraced an area of 120 acres. Such garden beds seem to be related to inclosures and should not be confused with the Indian cornfields of protohistoric times.

After about A.D. 700 the glory that was Hopewell was gone. The subsequent cultures of the Upper Great Lakes region seem to have been diversified outgrowths of a generalized Early Woodland and Middle Woodland base to which from time to time were added some exotic elements introduced from other regions.

REFERENCES | DEUEL, 1952; GIBSON, 1954; GOODE, 1937;
GREEN, 1954; GREENMAN, 1927, 1953;
QUIMBY, 1941a, 1941b, 1943a, 1943b, 1944, field notes.

10. CULTURAL DIVERSITY IN LATE

WOODLAND TIMES

A.D. 800–1600

The Late Woodland period in the Upper Great Lakes region was a time of cultural diversity. Although this was manifested primarily in material things, the underlying pattern was essentially uniform. In the areas where the environment permitted agriculture, the Indians made their living by simple farming, hunting, fishing, and gathering. In the far northern areas of the region where the environment prohibited the raising of corn, squash, beans, and tobacco, the Indians lived by hunting, fishing, and gathering.

In Late Woodland times all of the Indians of the Upper Great Lakes region had the bow and arrow, dogs, pottery, dwellings made of a framework of poles covered with bark, skins, or mats, and other tools, weapons, utensils, and paraphernalia that performed similar functions despite differences in details. It is, however, the differences in details that characterize this period.

Whereas in earlier periods there were certainly differences in details, such differences were the result of a cultural peak, or climax, placing one group of Indians above others—analogous to a dominant nation at its peak of cultural glory. In Late Woodland times the situation was different. There seems to have been a number of separate groups or nations of equal cultural level coexisting, each different from the others in details of material culture.

These conditions seem to imply that there was no tribal group, political federation, or pan-region religion strong enough to dominate the Upper Great Lakes region at this time. Instead there was a number of different cultures or nations, developing more or less equally, each in a separate area of the region.

Although most of the cultures of this period seemed to have developed in situ, there were three instances of cultures entering the region from elsewhere.

The natural environment of the Upper Great Lakes region during the Late Woodland period was essentially that of modern times. There were minor fluctuations of climate, and perhaps of flora and fauna, but nothing comparable to the drastic changes of much earlier periods. Sometime around A.D. 1000, the climate became somewhat warmer than it had been, and this condition lasted until around 1300, when the climate became cooler, and remained so until about 1850. It was during this warm spell that three new groups or nations of Indians from more southerly areas entered the Upper Great Lakes region.

In the following pages there are brief descriptions of the cultures that developed *in situ* as well as those that entered the region during the Late Woodland period.

THE EFFIGY MOUND CULTURE

The prehistoric Indians responsible for the construction of the mysterious effigy mounds lived principally in the southern half of Wisconsin. Their habitat was a mixture of deciduous forest and prairie openings. In the part of Wisconsin within the limits of the Upper Great Lakes region Effigy Mound sites are distributed from the latitude of the city of Green Bay on the north to slightly below the Wisconsin-Illinois boundary on the south.

The effigy mounds for which this culture is named are unique. They are low mounds of earth, seldom more than four feet high and often several hundred feet in length, shaped to represent various animals and birds (Fig. 43). The animal and bird effigy mounds occur in groups, along with low circular mounds and linear mounds.

These large groups of mounds were the cemeteries and ceremonial places of the Effigy Mound Indians. The dead were placed in pits or on prepared floors and covered by the mounds. In the animal and bird effigy mounds, burials were placed at focal points such as the head or heart; in circular mounds, burials were located in the center; and in linear mounds the burials were aligned with the long axis of the mound. Some mounds did not contain any burials and others with or without burials contained fireplaces, probably for ceremonial fires.

There were several types of burials: (1) body in flexed position; (2) remains consisting of a bundle of bones probably gathered from a previous interment or from a scaffold burial; and (3) cremation. Burial offerings were sometimes present, but generally sparse.

The groups of mounds—effigy, linear, and circular—were usually aligned

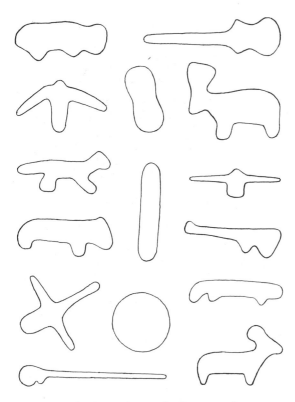

Fig. 43.—Outlines of typical effigy mounds

along the axis of some natural feature, such as a ridge or a lake shore, and the animal and bird forms seem to have been oriented purposefully within the group. Animal forms in profile and birds in full flight as seen from above are somewhat similar in style to the animal and bird representations painted on bark or wood by the Menomini and Dakota Indians of historic times.

Animal forms represented by effigy mounds are bear, deer, buffalo, canine (dog, fox, or wolf), and the mythical long-tailed panther. Bird forms probably were intended to represent eagles, hawks, ducks, and cranes. Circular and linear mounds, too, must have had some meaning to the Effigy Mound Indians.

It seems probable that all of the mounds erected by these Indians had some religious significance. Perhaps they were totem symbols, or effigies of animals, birds, or mythical creatures in especial association with various groupings of Indians within a tribe. Such a hypothesis would account for the reasons why

Fig. 44.—Cord-marked pottery of the Effigy Mound culture

one particular Indian would be buried beneath a bear effigy mound and another cremated and covered by an eagle-like mound of earth, and still another buried beneath a circular mound.

The Effigy Mound culture developed in Wisconsin. It came into being about A.D. 700 or 800 and lasted until about 1300. Its ancestry is still obscure and what happened to it is yet a mystery. However, one would guess that the Effigy Mound culture was ancestral to some Siouan group, such as the Dakota or some Algonkian group like the Menomini of the historic period.

Although there is no direct evidence, the Effigy Mound people probably practiced simple farming, along with hunting, fishing, and gathering, to obtain their livelihood. The area they lived in was suitable for farming, and simple agriculture had been introduced into the Upper Great Lakes region hundreds of years earlier.

The pottery of the Effigy Mound Indians consisted of open-mouth jars with wide shoulders and semiconoidal bases made of fired clay tempered with particles of granitic rock (Fig. 44). Vessel surfaces were roughened with imprints of a cord-wrapped paddle or partly smoothed after such roughening. Decoration confined to the shoulder or rim consisted of simple angular or linear designs, usually produced by cord-impressing and punctating and sometimes by stamping and incising.

The Effigy Mound people used stemmed and notched arrowpoints of chipped flint, antler arrowpoints, side-scrapers and end-scrapers of chipped flint; barbed harpoon points of bone, copper awls, flint drills, spatulate celts or spuds of ground stone (Fig. 45), copper wedges or axes, celts or ungrooved axes of ground stone, bone awls, stone "saws," beamers or hide-scraping tools of bone, and antler tools for chipping flint.

Ornaments were rare. There were, however, necklaces of hemispherical beads made of anculosa shells.

Tobacco pipes of elbow type were made of fired clay and decorated with simple geometric designs.

Nothing is known of Effigy Mound dwellings. Probably these Indians lived in bark- or mat-covered wigwams.

PENINSULAR WOODLAND CULTURE

Peninsular Woodland culture was the product of Indians who lived in the upper peninsula of Michigan, coastal Wisconsin, including the Door Peninsula, and the lower peninsula of Michigan, particularly its western half. These Indians lived along the lakes, rivers, and streams and on the islands in Lake Michigan and northern Lake Huron. Their villages were small and probably only occupied seasonally. They lived in wigwams made of sapling poles covered with bark, skins, or mats.

Subsistence was obtained by hunting, fishing, and simple farming. Because of environmental differences, farming was most important in the warmer southern portions of their habitat, whereas hunting was most important in the north. But even under the best of environmental conditions farming probably did not produce more than one-half of the subsistence of these Peninsular Woodland tribes.

Bows and arrows were used for hunting. Arrows were tipped with triangular points of chipped flint (Fig. 46), notched points of chipped flint, or conical antler points equipped with sockets.

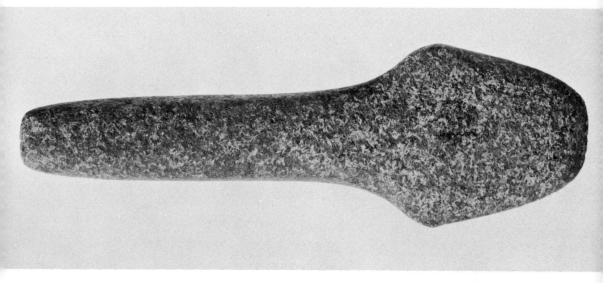

Fig. 45.—Spatulate celt of stone

For fishing there were bone fishhooks, spears tipped with harpoon-like points made of bone with a number of barbs on one side, nets, and notched stone sinkers.

They had clothing of animal skins. Bags were woven of twisted vegetal fiber or buffalo hair by means of twining techniques, and mats were made of reeds and rushes.

Various tools were ungrooved stone axes; occasionally small copper axes; bone awls; beaming tools or skin scrapers of bone; copper awls; drills of chipped flint; flaking tools of antler; variously formed scrapers of chipped flint; graving tools made of beaver incisors, sometimes hafted in antler tines; and knives of chipped flint.

Ornaments were simple and not particularly abundant. There were gorgets or breast ornaments of polished slate with usually two holes for suspension; beads made of thin flakes of copper rolled into short tubes; longer copper tubes used as hair ornaments (Figs. 47, 48); beads made of shell; beads made of sections of fossil crinoid stems, and circular breast ornaments of shell.

The Peninsular Woodland tribes made and used pottery. They had open-mouth jars with flaring or slightly flaring rims, constricted necks, and rounded or semiconoidal bottoms. Like all Indians of North America, they shaped their pottery by hand without the aid of a potter's wheel. Their pottery was

Fig. 46.—Triangular arrowheads of chipped flint from western Michigan

made of clay tempered with particles of granitic rock and, when completed, was fired to colors ranging from dark gray to light tan.

Exterior vessel surfaces were covered entirely by the imprints of a paddle-like object wrapped with twisted cord of two strands or were roughly smoothed subsequent to such treatment. Decoration, when present, was confined to the lip and rim and consisted of simple geometric patterns of linear elements produced by impressing with cords, cord-wrapped sticks, stick punches, and some tool that left impressions somewhat imitative of a cord-wrapped stick. Notched rims and lips were very popular in the latter half of the Late Woodland period (Fig. 49).

Fig. 47.—Hair ornaments of copper on skull with hair intact. This Peninsular Woodland burial was unusually well preserved.

Pottery was used for cooking and storage. In addition there were containers made of birchbark and probably bowls and ladles carved of wood.

Tobacco pipes usually were made of untempered clay fired to a gray or tan color (Fig. 50). Such pipes were of elbow type, made in one piece with bowl at right angle to the stem. Some of these pipes were plain. Others were decorated with simple patterns of incised lines or small punctates in rows. In rare instances sculptured animal effigies were added to the basic pipe form.

The Peninsular Woodland Indians buried their dead either in grave pits in cemeteries or beneath mounds of earth. There were primary burials with the bodies placed in a flexed position and secondary burials consisting of bundles

Fig. 48.—Reverse of skull shown in Figure 47

of bones representing a body either previously buried or one removed from a tree or scaffold where it had been placed shortly after death. There were also burials of cremated bones that probably were secondary burials. In some instances the bundle burials seem to have been wrapped in skin robes or birchbark.

All three types of burials occurred in mounds and in grave pits. All three types were also on occasion accompanied by grave offerings of tools, utensils, weapons, ornaments, and sometimes red ocher in lumps or in powdered form.

The mounds of the Peninsular Woodland tribes were usually dome-shaped and relatively small, about 15 to 50 feet in diameter, and seldom more than 4 feet high. Sometimes only single mounds occurred, but more often mounds were in groups of two to eight or perhaps more. Burials were placed in sub-

Fig. 49.—Fragments of Late Woodland pottery

floor pits near the center of the mound and at the floor or surrounding ground level within the mound.

The culture of the Peninsular Woodland tribes was relatively simple and uniform and widespread within the Upper Great Lakes region. It is this culture that seems to have been ancestral to the tribal cultures of the Menomini, Potawatomi, Ottawa, and Chippewa and perhaps Sauk and Fox.

MICHIGAN OWASCO CULTURE

The archeological remains of the Michigan Owasco culture are confined to southeastern Michigan and nearby parts of Ontario. In fact the Indian bearers of Michigan Owasco culture seem to have been easterners who entered southeastern Michigan from Ontario.

Fig. 50.—Tobacco pipes of fired clay from Late Woodland burial mound in western Michigan.

The Michigan Owasco Indians probably obtained more of their food by farming than they did by hunting and fishing. Vegetal foods were corn, beans, and squash (Fig. 51). Animal food included deer, beaver, bear, muskrat, marten, red fox, cottontail, gray squirrel, ruffed grouse, passenger pigeon, wild turkey, walleyed pike, largemouthed black bass, bullhead, catfish, perch, rock bass, northern pike, sheepshead, dogfish, turtles, and at least six species of mussels. Charred wood found in fire pits indicates that these Indians burned oak, ash, pine, maple, elm, and hickory in their cooking fires.

The Michigan Owasco Indians were short-statured people with relatively long heads. It is likely that they lived in rectangular cabins made of poles and covered with bark. Some villages probably were fortified with palisades, others were not thus protected. At one site there were two large ceremonial structures made of upright poles. The larger of these ceremonial structures was 585

Fig. 51.—Packets of pumpkin or squash seeds

feet long and 30 feet wide, the smaller was of the same width, but only half as long.

Tools and weapons of the Michigan Owasco Indians were made principally of stone, bone, and wood. Arrows were tipped with simple triangular points of chipped flint or notched points of chipped flint (Fig. 52). Various kinds of scrapers, drills, and knives were also of chipped flint. Ungrooved axes (celts) were made of ground and polished stone (Fig. 53). Awls and flaking tools were fabricated of bone and antler.

Tobacco pipes were of elbow type with obtuse- or right-angled bowls and short, thick stems. These pipes were made of fired clay and some of the pipe bowls were decorated with incised lines, punctates, or cord impressions arranged in simple linear patterns.

Michigan Owasco pottery ranged from small jars with globular bodies to

Fig. 52.—Late Woodland arrowheads and drills of chipped flint

large pots two feet high or more, with elongated bodies and round bottoms. Rims were straight or slightly flaring, usually weakly scalloped, and thickened in various ways, some of which resembled collared rims.

This pottery was made of fired clay tempered with particles of stone. The surfaces of vessels often had been coarsely smoothed; some were malleated with a cord-wrapped paddle.

Vessel decoration was somewhat more elaborate than that of the Peninsular Woodland Indians. Decoration confined to the rim, lip, and sometimes inner rim consisted of linear punctate, simple punctate and various stamped impressions, including cords and cord-wrapped sticks arranged in angular and

Fig. 53.—Ungrooved axes, or celts, of ground stone

linear patterns. Incised decoration was used sparingly. Pottery was utilitarian rather than ceremonial and used for cooking and storage.

The most unusual thing about the Michigan Owasco Indians was their treatment of the dead. Burial rites sometimes involving the use of the large ceremonial structures were apparently similar to the Huron feast of the dead (to be described subsequently). At certain times the bones of the deceased were gathered, cleaned, and rearticulated or bundled in skin robes, then carried in rituals performed in the ceremonial inclosure of upright poles, and finally buried.

The Michigan Owasco dead were buried in oblong or oval pits in cemeteries. There were flexed, bundle, and extended burials, as well as cremations and burials of isolated skulls and torsos. Many of the skulls had circular disks cut from the upper rear parts or had small holes drilled in them. Many of the long bones had perforations or were cut or grooved. Some of the skeletons placed in graves were completely rearticulated. In brief there had been post-mortem treatment of most of the bodies of the deceased. Some skeletons, perhaps those of husband and wife, were paired together in a single grave. Grave pits were sometimes lined with bark or with powdered red ocher. Grave goods were relatively rare.

The Michigan Owasco culture was the westernmost expression of an essentially eastern culture that in its early stages played an important role in the ancestry of Iroquoian culture. In its later stages some parts of Michigan Owasco may be ancestral Ottawa.

THE LALONDE CULTURE

The Lalonde culture of Ontario is well represented by sites in the northeastern portion of the Upper Great Lakes region. These sites are situated in Ontario in the area between Lake Huron and Georgian Bay and northward around Georgian Bay at least as far north as Lake Nipissing.

The Indian bearers of the Lalonde culture usually situated their village sites in inland positions, well removed from navigable water. Although direct information is lacking, it seems likely that these Indians lived in palisaded villages and had rectangular houses made of bark over a framework of poles.

The Lalonde Indians probably raised corn, beans, squash, and sunflowers for their seeds to be used as food. They also hunted with the bow and arrow and probably traps and snares. Available animals in the area included deer, elk, beaver, bear, woodchuck, muskrat, red squirrel, rabbit, raccoon, gray squirrel, chipmunk, fisher, lynx, wolf, skunk, and porcupine. Among the birds were passenger pigeon, ruffed grouse, wild turkey, Canada goose, crow, and raven. Snapping, wood, and painted turtles as well as walleyed pike, northern pike, catfish, sheepshead, and other fishes were also available.

Arrows were tipped with triangular, side-notched points of chipped flint or with points of bone and antler. Winged type drill points and various types of scrapers and knives were made of chipped flint. Ungrooved axes or adzes were made of ground and polished stone and awls were made of bone.

Ornaments were rare, but Lalonde Indians did have beads made of hollow bird bones.

Lalonde tobacco pipes were made of fired clay. Usually pipes were of right-angle elbow type with trumpet-shaped bowls. Less common were elbow pipes with barrel-shaped bowls. Some pipes were ornamented with simple incised or punctate designs.

Lalonde pottery consisted of open-mouthed jars with flaring, high-collared rims, elongated bodies, and round bottoms. Rims were sometimes castellated and jar mouths were sometimes angular.

Jars were made of fired clay that had been tempered with particles of stone. Vessel surfaces were very smooth and brown to light brown in color.

Decoration, usually confined to the wide rim collar, consisted of angular and rectilinear plats of parallel lines boldly incised with precision. Some jars made without high collars had a similarly decorated area encircling the body of the vessel.

Data are lacking on Lalonde burial customs. Probably they buried their dead in pits, and probably they had ossuaries, or mass burials.

The Lalonde culture may have been ancestral to historic eastern Iroquois and certainly was ancestral to western Iroquoian tribes, particularly the pre-historic Huron, who later lived in the same area.

It seems probable that Lalonde culture in its formative stage was influenced by southern cultures in the Mississippi Valley. In the Late Woodland period some southern cultures were moving northward and it would have been easy for southern traits to diffuse to the southwestern shores of Lake Erie and then to southwestern Ontario.

THE FISHER CULTURE

The ancient groups of Indians manifested by what archeologists call the Fisher culture, entered the Upper Great Lakes area from their original home-land in the Illinois River Valley. The Fisher culture, named for the owner of the land upon which was situated the first excavated site, came into being sometime after A.D. 1000 and subsequently spread northward into the Kanka-kee, Calumet, and St. Joseph River valleys of northeastern Illinois, north-western Indiana, and southwestern Michigan at about A.D. 1300 to 1400.

This area at the time of occupancy was a mixture of grassland and clusters of trees, primarily oak, with some extensive areas of swampland and marsh on the lakeward borders. The Indian occupants of the area tended to place their villages and cemeteries on sandy terraces and beaches, fossil remnants of the

Fig. 54.—Artifacts of stone and bone: triangular arrowheads of chipped flint, a socketed arrowhead of antler, bone awls, assorted scrapers of chipped flint, a sandstone shaft-smoother, and two flint drills.

glacial and postglacial lake stages, or upon old river terraces, all of which were open, well-drained places.

The Indian carriers of the Fisher culture made their living by farming and hunting. They raised corn, squash, beans, and tobacco. Cultivation was by simple digging stick and hoes made of mussel shells or the shoulder blades of deer, bison, and elk attached to wooden handles. The bow and arrow was used for hunting. Arrows made of wood, smoothed by grooved sandstone polishers used in pairs, were tipped with small triangular points made of chipped flint or with socketed antler points (Figs. 54, 55). Fishhooks of bone and shell and probably spears and nets were used for catching fish. Remains from refuse pits in Cook County, Illinois, sites show that the following animals were utilized:

Fig. 55.—Pottery, an ungrooved ax of stone, socketed arrow-heads made of antler, a bone awl, and two arrow shaft smoothers of sandstone.

buffalo, elk, deer, bear, wolf, otter, mink, muskrat, beaver, badger, raccoon, skunk, bobcat, lynx, squirrel, rabbit, and chipmunk. Among the birds taken were ducks, eagles, herons, cranes, wild turkeys, swans, grouse, geese, passenger pigeons, hawks, and prairie chickens. There were several varieties of turtles and mussels as well as the following fish: bowfin, bullhead, buffalo fish, sucker, channel catfish, northern pike, and freshwater drum.

The only domesticated animal was the dog.

The Fisher people lived in rectangular houses made of upright poles set into the ground and probably covered with bark or mats.

These Indians made and used lots of pottery, some of which was rather ornate. The common forms were globular jars with round bottoms and flaring rims (Fig. 55). Some jars had strap handles at the rim level. Decoration consisted of cord impressions, broad trailed lines, and punctates in chevrons, festoons, and geometric plats around the shoulder and rim areas of the vessels. The outer edges of the rims were frequently ornamented by crimping, grooving, or notching. This pottery was made of clay tempered with particles of shell or with particles of granitic rock, and vessel surfaces were either smooth or roughened by cord-wrapped paddles.

Tobacco pipes were made of stone and had separate stems of wood or bone. Some pipes were vase-shaped, others were small, equal-armed elbow types.

Among the tools in common use were ungrooved axes of stone, needles and awls of bone, knives, and scrapers of chipped flint, beamers or fleshing tools made of deer leg bones, stone paint grinders, and tapered drills of chipped flint (Figs. 54, 55).

Ornaments included beads, pendants, and ear ornaments of shell; small tubular beads of rolled sheet copper; ear ornaments of wood covered with thin sheet copper, and beads made of bird bone.

Musical instruments were the turtle-shell rattle, the rasp made of notched bone, probably drums, and probably flutes and whistles of bone.

Burials usually were in cemeteries on sandy ridges or terraces. Deceased persons were placed, extended on the back, in oblong, shallow pits. Tools, weapons, utensils, and ornaments were often placed in the graves. In one instance the remains of an otter-skin medicine bag adorned with copper was found in a site in Cook County, Illinois. This medicine bag probably was similar to some of those found among Indians of the Upper Great Lakes region in historic times.

The Fisher culture developed in the Illinois River Valley and was based upon a southern type of culture from the Mississippi Valley that had moved northward during the warm period that began about A.D. 1000. This is reflected in the changing styles of Fisher ceramics. Their earliest pottery was most ornate, with smooth vessel surfaces and shell-tempering in the clay. The late pottery was simple in decoration, often grit-tempered, and frequently vessel surfaces were roughened by means of a cord-wrapped paddle.

About A.D. 1300, perhaps slightly later, some Fisher people left the Illinois Valley and established themselves in the southern part of the Upper Great Lakes region. The Fisher culture must have been the ancestor of one of the Central Algonkian tribes, probably the Miami, who will be mentioned in greater detail subsequently.

THE LAKE WINNEBAGO CULTURE

The remains of the Lake Winnebago culture have been found in northeastern Wisconsin in the area around Lake Winnebago and from there northward to the tip of Door County, the peninsula separating Green Bay from Lake Michigan.

The bearers of the Lake Winnebago culture were the ancestors of the Winnebago Indians who occupied the same area at the time of its discovery by Europeans. These ancestral Winnebago entered the Upper Great Lakes region around A.D. 1000, and they came from somewhere in the Upper Mississippi Valley and its tributaries, perhaps by way of Aztalan. Moreover, Lake Winnebago culture is known only from archeological research, despite the fact that Winnebago tribal culture of the seventeenth century and later has been described by historians and ethnologists.

The Lake Winnebago Indians made their living by farming and hunting. They raised corn, squash, beans, and tobacco. They hunted local animals, such as the elk, deer, bear, wolf, fox, beaver, raccoon, otter, mink, muskrat, woodchuck, squirrel, and rabbit. They also took various birds and fish and collected mussels, hickory nuts, butternuts, and hazel nuts.

They hunted with the bow and arrow and probably used traps and snares also. Arrow shafts were smoothed by sanding or grinding them between paired tablets of sandstone with matching longitudinal grooves. Arrows were tipped with triangular points of chipped flint or with socketed antler points. Fish were taken with bone hooks, spears tipped with detachable bone points with multiple barbs on one side only, and with nets. Small fish effigies of shell were probably used as lures when spearing fish.

The Lake Winnebago people made their tools of bone, stone, and wood. They had ungrooved axes of ground and polished granitic stone, side and end scrapers of chipped flint, mussel-shell scrapers, rather thick elliptical scrapers of chipped flint, flaking tools of antler, knives or scrapers of sharpened flint flakes, knives of chipped flint, several kinds of bone awls, tapered drills of chipped flint, and fleshing or beaming tools made of deer leg bones.

Ornaments included beads or tubes of bird bone, either plain or engraved with simple geometric motifs of linear elements; pendants of stone, sheet copper, and shell; and beads of thin sheet copper rolled into tubes.

Tobacco pipes were made of polished stone, usually of catlinite, but occasionally of soapstone and sandstone. All of these pipes were of the disk-shaped variety.

Fig. 56.—Shell spoon

Fig. 57.—Pottery of the Lake Winnebago culture (After McKern)

Utensils included spoons of mussel shell with notched handles (Fig. 56), mussel-shell ladles with wooden handles, wooden bowls and ladles, and pottery.

Lake Winnebago pottery (Fig. 57) was made of fired clay that had been tempered with particles of crushed mussel shell. Among the various large and small forms of vessels were globular pots with round bottoms, hemispherical bowls, and tall, slender vessels. The rims of pots were flaring, some to a pronounced degree, and loop handles were common.

Vessel surfaces were hard and smooth and usually ornamented with broadly incised or trailed lines and punctates. Designs, confined to the upper halves of vessels, consisted of horizontal, vertical, or diagonal plats of parallel lines and punctates.

Small disks made from sherds of broken vessels by grinding the edges probably were counters in a game of some kind. Some of these disks were perforated at their centers.

The Lake Winnebago Indians buried their dead in oblong grave pits in cemeteries. The deceased generally were extended full length on their backs in the burial pits. Tools, weapons, utensils, and ornaments were placed with the dead for their use in the spirit world.

THE BLUE ISLAND CULTURE

Archeological remains indicative of the Blue Island culture have been found only in the Chicago area at sites in the southern part of Cook County, Illinois. The Blue Island culture was similar to the Lake Winnebago culture and probably represents an ancient occupancy of the Chicago area by one of the Chiwere Siouan groups, perhaps an offshoot of the ancestral Iowa, Oto, or Missouri in the period from about A.D. 1300 to 1600.

At the time of occupancy the area was prairie grassland, with rare clusters of deciduous trees and some swamps. This was part of an extension of the prairie grasslands from west of the Mississippi River into the Chicago area, the only appreciable part of the Upper Great Lakes region that was not forested.

The Blue Island culture was the product of Indians who lived by farming and hunting. They lived in rectangular houses made of upright poles set into the ground and probably covered with woven mats. Such houses ranged in size from 25 by 10 feet to 55 by 15 feet.

Pottery was shell-tempered with smooth surfaces and decoration on shoul-

Fig. 58.—Stone pipe bowl with face carved on it.

Fig. 59.—Engraved gorget, or breast ornament, of marine shell.

der areas of straight lines narrowly incised or broadly trailed, sometimes combined with punctate impressions and arranged in vertical or slanting groups. Vessels were round-bottom pots with wide mouths and outslanting rims that were crimped, grooved, or notched along the lip. Strap handles joining rim and upper shoulder were ornamented with incised lines and punctate decorations.

Weapons, tools, ornaments, and tobacco pipes closely resembled those of the Fisher and Lake Winnebago cultures. One effigy pipe (Fig. 58), probably once equipped with a stem made from a portion of human leg bone, indicates relationships with Iroquoian peoples in Canada.

Cultural traits that seem to have been rare were the grooved, biconical club head of ground stone, the small masklike gorget of marine shell with engraved weeping eye motif (Fig. 59), and a bird effigy of carved bone.

Burial practices were essentially the same as those described for the Fisher and Lake Winnebago cultures. In one site, the remains of what probably were medicine bags made of mink and bobcat were found with a burial.

SUMMARY OF LATE WOODLAND PERIOD—A.D. 800–1600

All of these different cultures of the Late Woodland period coexisted and developed, each in its own environment, in the Upper Great Lakes region. The

Effigy Mound culture occupied the prairie transition and the deciduous forest zone of southern hardwoods and northeastern hardwoods in Wisconsin. The Peninsular Woodland culture preferred a forest zone composed of northeastern pines or hardwoods in northern Wisconsin, Michigan, and Ontario. The Michigan Owasco culture was confined to the forest band of southern hardwoods and the transition zone of northeastern hardwoods in southeastern Michigan and adjacent portions of Ontario.

The Lalonde culture occupied the southern hardwood forest of southwestern Ontario and the carriers of the Fisher culture preferred the transition zone of prairie grassland and southern hardwood forest. The Lake Winnebago people occupied the northeastern hardwood forest near its border with the southern hardwood forest in eastern Wisconsin, and the Blue Island Indians lived in the prairie grassland of the Chicago area.

With three exceptions all of these cultures evolved from ancestral groups already resident in the Upper Great Lakes region. The Fisher, Lake Winnebago, and Blue Island cultures underwent development after entering the Upper Great Lakes region from the valleys of the Mississippi and its tributaries.

It is quite likely that some groups of Indians, once resident in the Upper Great Lakes had left the region by A.D. 1600. However, the tribes found by European explorers in the Upper Great Lakes region after A.D. 1600 were all descended from various Late Woodland cultures that had occupied the region previously.

The tribal cultures found in the region after A.D. 1600 are described in the following chapters.

REFERENCES

BLUHM and WENNER, 1956;

Collections and notes in Chicago Natural History Museum;

Collections in Oshkosh Public Museum;

GREENMAN, 1937, 1939, 1953; GRIFFIN, 1943, 1958;

GUTHE, field notes; HINSDALE, 1929, 1930; KIDD, 1952, 1954;

LEE, 1951, 1952, 1958; LISS and BLUHM, 1958;

McKERN, 1928, 1930, 1942, 1945; MEYER, 1952;

QUIMBY, field notes; RIDLEY, 1952a, 1952b, 1954, 1958;

ROWE, 1956; WINTEMBERG, 1946; WRAY, 1952.

11. INDIAN TRIBES OF THE EARLY

HISTORIC PERIOD

A.D. 1600–1760

The Indian tribes of the Upper Great Lakes region during the Early Historic period were the Huron, Ottawa, Chippewa or Ojibwa, Potawatomi, Winnebago, Menomini, Sauk, Fox, and Miami (see map, Fig. 60). These at least are the tribes that would have been counted by the first census taker, had there been one in the region at the time.

There were no census takers, but from the reports and diaries of European explorers, missionaries, and fur traders estimates of population have been obtained, and these provide the basis for the first census of the Upper Great Lakes region.

There were 45,000 to 60,000 Indians in the Huron-Tionontati tribes; 3,000 to 3,500 Ottawa Indians; some 25,000 to 35,000 Indians among the various bands of the Chippewa tribe; 4,000 Potawatomi Indians; 3,800 persons in the Winnebago tribe; 3,000 Menomini Indians; 3,500 Sauk Indians; 3,000 Fox Indians, and 4,500 persons in the Miami tribe.

These estimates suggest that there was a population of at least 100,000 Indians occupying the Upper Great Lakes region at the beginning of the Early Historic period.

In the Upper Great Lakes region there are about 144,000 square miles of land and inland lakes.

A population of about 100,000 persons occupying and using about 144,000 square miles of land and inland lakes and rivers suggests a population density of less than one person per square mile. This certainly was not a dense population judged by modern standards, but it may have been considered so in terms of the standards of the Indian occupants. After all, about 10 per cent of the prehistoric owners of North America north of Mexico seem to have lived in the Upper Great Lakes region.

The greatest population density in the Upper Great Lakes region seems to

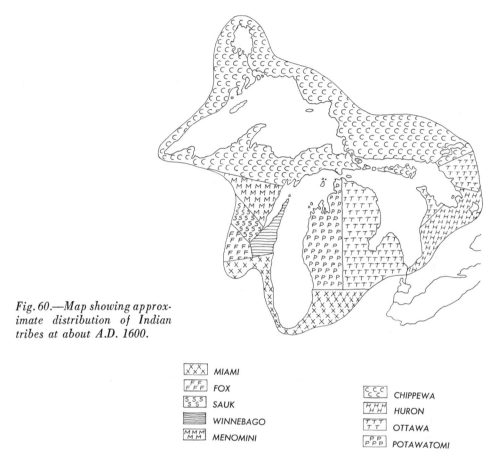

Fig. 60.—Map showing approximate distribution of Indian tribes at about A.D. 1600.

MIAMI

FOX

SAUK

WINNEBAGO

MENOMINI

CHIPPEWA

HURON

OTTAWA

POTAWATOMI

have been in Ontario, in the region between Lake Simcoe and Georgian Bay and the adjacent land westward and southwestward to Lake Huron. In A.D. 1600 this area was the homeland of the Huron and Tionontati people. Within this area of perhaps 4,500 square miles, there probably lived at least 45,000 Indians, a population density of ten persons per square mile.

The most sparse population density seems to have been in the Lake Superior basin of upper Michigan and Ontario. In this area there were perhaps some 20,000 Chippewa using an area of about 49,000 square miles, a population density of less than one person per two square miles.

These differences in density of population within the Upper Great Lakes region reflect the subsistence level and the limitations of environment. The highest density of population was found among Indians who obtained their subsistence by farming and did relatively little hunting. Under these conditions the least amount of land would support the most people.

The lowest density of population was found in the northern parts of the region where farming was impossible. Here the Indians obtained their subsistence by hunting and the size of the population was geared directly to the size of the animal population in a predator-prey relationship.

In other parts of the Upper Great Lakes region there were tribes of Indians who gained their subsistence by a combination of farming and hunting in almost equal parts. Their population densities varied in relation to the size of the areas they utilized for hunting. If measured only in terms of their villages and farm lands they would have had a relatively high density of population. Their relatively low population densities were as much a measure of the territory they were able to control as a measure of subsistence level.

Each of the Indian tribes in the Upper Great Lakes region had its own language and each of these languages belonged to one of three major language families or stocks, Iroquoian, Algonkian, or Siouan.

The language of the Hurons belonged to the Iroquoian family of languages. The Winnebago language belonged to the Chiwere division of the Siouan linguistic stock. All of the other tribes in the Upper Great Lakes region possessed languages belonging to the Algonkian family.

Chippewa and Ottawa were dialects of essentially the same Algonkian language. Potawatomi, although a separate language, was closer to Chippewa-Ottawa than to any other Algonkian language. Menomini, although separate, seems to have been most closely related to the Sauk and Fox (with Kickapoo) group of Algonkian dialects. The Miami, along with the Illinois, who lived south of the Upper Great Lakes region, formed another linguistic division of the Algonkian family.

Upon the basis of linguistic relationships there was the following grouping of tribes within the Upper Great Lakes region: The Huron stood alone; the Ottawa, Chippewa, and Potawatomi formed a group of related tribes; the Winnebago stood alone; the Menomini, Sauk, and Fox (and Kickapoo on the western edge of the region) formed a group of related tribes; and the Miami (with the Illinois to the south of them) were a separate group.

In terms of social organization, particularly the systems of classifying relatives and regulating marriage and inheritance, there were significant groupings of tribal cultures within the Upper Great Lakes region. These groupings are as follows:

The Huron, Chippewa, Ottawa, and Potawatomi formed one group in terms of their common system of classifying relatives and regulating marriage. However, the Huron reckoned descent in the female line—they were matrilineal, whereas the Chippewa, Ottawa, and Potawatomi were patrilineal. Thus the Chippewa, Ottawa, and Potawatomi form one group and the Huron, though similar, constitute a separate grouping.

The other tribes of the Upper Great Lakes, the Winnebago, Menomini, Sauk and Fox, Miami, and their neighboring tribes to the south and west of the region have in common a different system of classifying relations and regulating marriage, and thus comprise a third grouping.

Another way to classify these various tribes of Indians is by their modes of subsistence. The Hurons were intensive farmers and engaged in a limited amount of hunting, primarily to obtain raw materials for clothing and tools. The Chippewa, on the other hand, were essentially hunters. The rest of the Upper Great Lakes tribes had a subsistence based about equally upon farming and hunting. The Menomini, however, combined their farming with the gathering of wild rice, probably to a greater degree than any other tribe in the region.

Those tribes oriented toward the southern and southwestern parts of the region, the Sauk, Fox, and Miami, undertook communal hunts in the prairies. The northern tribes, such as the Ottawa and Potawatomi who hunted in the forests, separated into small family groups when hunting. The Winnebago and Menomini seem to have been intermediate.

All of the tribes in the Upper Great Lakes, except the nomadic Chippewa, were essentially sedentary. And even the Chippewa tended to congregate in larger groups in summer, especially at favorable fishing placs.

The arrival of European explorers, fur traders, and missionaries in the Upper Great Lakes region was responsible for a number of changes in the native tribal cultures. In the period from 1600 to 1760 this culture change was not as rapid as it was later. The first changes were in relation to material things such as weapons, tools, and utensils.

Iron knives were substituted for stone knives, iron hoes replaced wooden and bone or shell hoes, iron axes were substituted for stone axes, and iron and brass points replaced the chipped-stone points on arrows.

French type bastions and gates were added to the aboriginal type of wooden stockades, and brass kettles were introduced to compete with pottery vessels of native manufacture.

Porcelain beads in abundance were preferred to the old beads of marine shell, and brass rings and bracelets were worn by the women. Lengths of French sword blades were hafted to wooden spears instead of shorter blades of chipped flint. Guns were introduced and used along with bows and arrows.

French clothing came to have value in terms of prestige and was worn for show on top of the native clothing made of animal skins. Even some food plants, such as peas and watermelons, were introduced by the French, who also were responsible for the addition of house cats, pigs, geese, ducks, and chickens. Pigs came to be used at feasts in place of especially fattened bears and dogs.

In non-material aspects of culture the changes were not particularly great. Religion was the cultural field of greatest interest to the missionaries, and change in religious ideas was very slow. Some inroads were made, however, because as early as 1679 some remnants of the Huron gave a dance at Christmas to celebrate the birth of Christ and his arrival at their village.

The changes in tribal culture were earlier in the eastern part of the Upper Great Lakes region than they were in the western and northern portions; for it was there that the Indians first encountered the Europeans. Moreover, in much of this period the quantity of goods introduced was not sufficient to cause the Indian to abandon his old handicrafts. The old and the new persisted until near the end of the period, at which time some of the old handicrafts became extinct through lack of use. By 1760 pottery-making had ceased and brass kettles were used almost exclusively. Guns had finally replaced the bow and arrow, and wars and the fur trade had brought about a number of changes in the various tribal cultures.

In the following chapters are described the tribal cultures as they existed before any of these changes had taken place—the tribal cultures of the Upper Great Lakes as they were when first encountered in the region by the advancing Europeans.

REFERENCES   HOIJER, 1946; KINIETZ, 1940; KROEBER, 1939; QUIMBY, 1939.

12. THE HURON AND THE CHIPPEWA

A.D. 1600–1760

THE HURON—A.D. 1600–50

The Huron and their close relatives, the Tionontati or Tobacco Huron, lived in Ontario between Lake Simcoe and Georgian Bay and westward of Lake Simcoe to Lake Huron. The combined Huron and Tobacco Huron are estimated to have had a population of 45,000 to 60,000 persons at the beginning of the seventeenth century. However, by the middle of the century their numbers had been reduced drastically by introduced diseases, war, and famine, and the tribal remnants had been driven from their homeland.

The Hurons lived in towns and villages, some of which were protected by circular palisades 15 to 35 feet high, made of upright logs in three rows and equipped with galleries and watchtowers. Within the towns and villages, houses were arranged in regular rows along streets and separated from one another for protection against fire. One of the largest of the Huron towns, Cahiagné, contained two hundred large dwellings in which lived 4,000 to 6,000 persons.

The large houses were 150 feet to 180 feet long, 36 feet wide, and 24 feet high. They were made of poles about 8 inches thick united into a strong frame and covered with slabs of bark from such trees as elm, ash, and cedar. Running lengthwise through the middle of the house there was a passage 10 or 12 feet wide. Around the interior walls was a sleeping platform 4 feet high covered with woven mats.

Each house was divided into compartments for individual families related to each other through the female line. The large houses contained about twenty families sharing 10 fires in the middle aisle, and the smallest houses had six families sharing 3 fires. Probably the average house contained ten families sharing 5 fires.

Within the houses were kept the personal belongings of the occupants, woven mats for sitting and sleeping, cooking utensils, and bark chests with the year's supply of corn, and firewood for heating the houses in winter.

Firewood was exceedingly important. Only very dry, relatively smokeless wood was burned in the houses. As the easily accessible sources of firewood became exhausted in a period of seven to twelve years it was necessary to move the towns and villages at least three-quarters of a mile closer to the source of firewood. In some instances the old villages were left standing.

Within each village there was at least one council house, larger than any of the regular dwellings.

The Hurons and the Tobacco Hurons obtained their food by farming. In the cleared fields near their towns and villages they raised corn, beans, squashes, and sunflowers for sustenance, and tobacco for smoking. The men cleared the land of trees and brush by cutting and burning, but the women planted the food crops, tended the fields, and did the harvesting.

Selected seed corn was soaked several days, then planted nine or ten grains to the hole at three-foot intervals. Digging sticks and wooden hoes were the only agricultural implements. The corn ripened in three to four months and was harvested. Each cornstalk, high as a man, had two or three ears and each ear contained two to three hundred kernels. It has been estimated that the Huron alone harvested 390,000 bushels of corn annually and that they had 23,300 acres of corn under cultivation. There must have been miles of fields surrounding the Huron villages. So extensive were these fields that one French missionary got lost in them while walking from one village to another.

Corn was prepared for eating in some twenty to forty different ways. Types of bread were made from corn pounded into meal in large wooden mortars with long, heavy pestles of wood. Fish, bear, and deer fat was used to flavor a number of corn dishes.

Squashes were also an important crop. The women forced sprouting of the seeds by placing them in bark containers filled with moist powdered wood from rotted logs and suspending them over a fire. In a few days the seeds sprouted and were then planted in prepared fields.

As a subsistence activity, hunting was relatively unimportant among the Huron and Tobacco Huron. Both hunting and fishing combined produced about one-quarter or less of the food consumed annually. Except in some ceremonial circumstances, meat and fish were used primarily in corn recipes to give added flavor. Yet hunting was necessary to provide skins for the manufacture of clothing. The Huron system of hunting deer was analogous to a cattle roundup. The Indians methodically covered the area to be hunted, frightening and driving the deer into previously prepared triangular inclosures

*Fig. 61.—Huron women and man in rod armor, as pictured by
seventeenth-century European artist.*

more than 3,000 feet long on a side, made of upright posts 8 or 9 feet high. Within these inclosures the deer were killed with arrows and spears.

Hunting alone did not provide the number of animal skins required annually by the Hurons. The additional skins of deer and beaver were obtained by trade from tribes dwelling north or south of the Huron. Corn, shell beads called wampum, and fish nets were the articles exchanged for the animal skins. Such trade was a formal activity among the Huron and was only undertaken by specialists who inherited or otherwise acquired special rights and privileges to engage in trade.

Fishing was much more important than hunting. Fish were taken both in summer and in winter. They were caught with spears, hooks and lines, and long gill nets equipped with weights and floats. The Huron had fishing camps on the shores and islands of Georgian Bay in Lake Huron. Fish oil and dried fish were important additions to their corn and bean dishes.

The Hurons had no domesticated animal except the dog. Fattened dogs were eaten at special feasts. Bears kept in captivity for several years of fattening were also eaten at feasts.

Both men and women wore clothing made of the skins of deer, bear, and beaver. Both sexes wore mocassins, leggings, and robes. The men wore breech clouts and shirts with detached sleeves. The women wore skirts reaching to their knees (Fig. 61) and shirts in winter, but nothing above the waist in summer. Clothing was decorated with painted bands of red and brown.

Women wore their hair well-combed, oiled, and arranged in a single tress hanging down the back and tied with eelskins. Men wore their hair in a variety of ways. Some shaved half of the head, many left the hair long and hanging, others left a strip of hair running along the midline of the head.

Most of the men painted their faces and bodies with a variety of designs, mostly in black and red but also in green and violet. The pigment obtained from mineral and vegetal sources was mixed with sunflower oil and bear fat. Some men, particularly among the Tobacco Huron, tattooed their bodies with representations of animals.

The women were not painted or tattooed, but wore necklaces and chains of shell beads around their necks and waists and hanging down in front of their robes and skirts.

Huron weapons used in hunting and/or warfare were the bow and arrow, spear, and wooden club. Arrows were tipped with conical points of antler or with triangular points of chipped stone. Spears were equipped with chipped

Fig. 62.—Huron pottery from northeastern Georgian Bay

stone blades. In warfare the Huron men used armor made of wooden slats and wickerwork shields covered with rawhide (Fig. 61).

Ungrooved axes of ground stone, chipped flint knives, and various types of scrapers and awls and fish nets were made by the Huron men. The Huron women made the clothing, wove mats, made baskets and containers of bark, took care of the children, spun bast fiber into twine, prepared the food, and made pottery.

Huron pottery was smooth and hard, made of clay tempered with particles of grit and fired to a reddish buff or gray color (Fig. 62). The common vessels were globular jars with round bottoms and short, flaring rims, sometimes with flat-topped projections or castellations. There were a number of variations, including jars with elliptical orifices and handles. Decoration was confined to the shoulder and rim exteriors and consisted of linear and angular plats of short incised lines and punctate impressions combined in encircling zones.

Tobacco pipes made of fired clay or polished stone were in common use. Shapes were variable and included elbow pipes, trumpet shapes, and vase-shaped pipes. Less common were effigy forms representing humans, birds, and animals. The vase-shaped pipes were used with added stems of bone, reed, or wood. Clay pipes were often ornamented with incised lines and punctate impressions.

Huron travel generally was on foot, aided in winter by the use of snowshoes. The Huron towns and villages were usually situated inland away from waterways navigable by canoe. Nonetheless, the Hurons made and used birchbark canoes of the same style as their Algonkian-speaking neighbors to the north. Such canoes were particularly useful in their fishing activities along the shores of Lake Huron in Georgian Bay.

Burdens were transported on their own backs with the aid of a tumpline. With suitable snow in winter, burdens were transported by toboggans.

Huron social organization was somewhat elaborate and of a type to be expected in terms of their well-developed technology. The Hurons were divided into bands, villages, clans, and families.

A Huron clan was a group of relatives tracing their descent through the female line from a hypothetical, single ancestor. Each Huron was a member of one and only one of these matrilineal clans. A person could not marry a member of the same clan. Therefore, of any given family a mother and her children belonged to one clan and the father belonged to a different clan.

Each of the Huron long houses sheltered up to twenty-four related women of the same clan, each with her children and her husband. Thus the houses were in effect clan houses and the married men lived in the houses of their wives. Probably in each town and village houses belonging to women of the same clan were grouped together.

Representing each clan were one or more chiefs, who seem to have held their position by hereditary right. At the death of a chief his name and position passed to his sister's son, a male of his own clan. The clan chiefs within a town comprised a town council that met with the town chief to decide civil matters. The town chieftainship probably was hereditary within a specific lineage and clan.

Towns and villages in groups formed bands. There were four bands for the Huron proper. These were the Rock, Cord, Bear, and Deer bands. The Bear band seems to have been the largest and most powerful of the Huron bands. It had fourteen towns and villages in 1638.

Each band had a chief, who, with the aid of a council composed of village and town chiefs, handled civil affairs of interest to the entire band. In matters involving the entire Huron tribe, or nation, there was a meeting of band chiefs and their councils. Such meetings were held in the village of the particular band chief who had asked for the meeting.

The religious life of the Huron, although not so elaborate in structure as the political and social organization, was nevertheless somewhat more elaborated than that of their Algonkian-speaking neighbors.

The Hurons believed that the world, as they knew it, was perched on the back of a giant turtle. The sun at night disappeared into a tunnel in the earth and came out at the opposite end each morning.

The supernatural creator of the world and of the Huron people was named Yoscaha. He was a benevolent spirit who lived in the sky. His grandmother, Ataensiq, seems to have been an evil spirit. There was also a class of numerous spirits called Oki who had power for both good and evil. The Oki were present in rivers, rocks, places, animals, and situations such as voyages, fishing trips, trade, war, and ceremonial feasts. The Oki seem to have been expressions of a power similar to the manito of the Algonkian-speaking peoples. The power of the Oki was also present in amulets and charms of various kinds kept by the Hurons. The Oki manifested themselves to individuals human beings in dreams. The Hurons believed that dreams were the language of the soul.

The soul, according to the Huron, had five aspects or conditions of being. It animated the body and gave it life. It was possessed of reason. It enabled thinking and deliberation. It made possible affection for others. And it separated itself from the body after death.

The Hurons believed that souls, after death, went to various villages of souls in the sky. These soul villages of the Huron afterworld were devoid of reward or punishment and supernatural life in them was essentially the same as natural life on earth.

Some souls after death followed the Milky Way, the road of souls, to a great soul village toward the setting sun. They journeyed together, dressed in fine robes and carrying their equipage, all taken with them in soul form from their common grave.

Other souls, such as those of very old people and young children not capable of a long journey, traveled to a different soul village less distant. Souls of Hurons killed in war also had a separate village.

Souls did not go to their respective soul villages until after an elaborate mass burial ceremony known as the Feast of the Dead.

Ordinarily when a Huron died his corpse was placed in a bark coffin raised on painted wooden posts nine or ten feet high, but those killed in war or drowned were buried in a flexed position in shallow graves. Souls of all these Indians remained in the vicinity of the Huron villages. Infants were buried in the roads between villages so that their souls might enter passing women and be born again.

The Feast of the Dead (Fig. 63) was held at eight-, ten-, or twelve-year intervals. It was a national ceremony at which all of the dead from each Huron town were removed from their temporary graves and brought to a designated place for mass burial.

In preparation for the Feast of the Dead the living Indians of each town and village removed the bodies from their temporary graves. The bones were lovingly stripped of remaining flesh and/or cleaned by relatives and mourners of the deceased. An eyewitness account from the missionary Brébeuf in 1636 states:

—having opened the graves, they display—all these corpses,—long enough for the spectators to learn—what they will be some day. The flesh of some is quite gone, and there is only parchment on their bones; in other cases, the bodies look as if they had been dried and smoked, and show scarcely any signs of putrefaction; and in still other cases they are still swarming with worms,—finally, after some time they strip them of their flesh, taking off the skin and flesh (by handfuls) which they throw into the fire along with robes and mats in which the bodies were wrapped.

After being stripped of flesh, the bones were placed in beaver-skin bags or rearticulated and dressed in fine robes and adorned with bracelets and strings of beads. Some bags of bones were arranged to form human effigies that were ornamented with strings of beads and bands of long fur dyed red.

The bodies from each town and village having been prepared, they were then transported on the backs of the villagers to the spot designated for the mass burial. This was a ceremonial journey purposely drawn out two or three days.

At the place selected for burial, there was a large pit 30 feet to 60 feet square and up to 10 feet deep. At the edge of the pit was a high scaffold or

Fig. 63.—The Feast of the Dead as pictured by a European engraver of the early eighteenth century.

platform. Bodies were hung from poles on this scaffold and bundles of bones were placed on the platform. After lengthy ceremonies and rituals in which the whole Huron nation participated, the bodies were placed in the pit along with beautiful fur robes, pottery, weapons, tools, ornaments, food, and utensils.

Hundreds of people were thus buried and thousands of useful articles were lavished upon the dead. At the end of the Feast of the Dead the souls of the Hurons buried in this way departed from Huronia and went to the various soul villages in the sky.

Such elaborate burial rituals and such lavishing of wealth upon the dead is reminiscent of Hopewell death rites practiced more than a thousand years earlier in the Upper Great Lakes region. It is quite probable that Huron death rituals perpetuated a part of the religious tradition that once had been Hopewellian.

THE CHIPPEWA—A.D. 1640–1760

The Chippewa (also called Ojibwa) Indians lived in the forested lands draining into Lake Superior and northern Lake Huron. Within this vast area there were many independent bands of Chippewa, totaling about 25,000 or more Indians.

Unlike the Huron, the Chippewa were for the most part nomadic hunters, although a few bands in favorable situations practiced a rudimentary form of agriculture, in addition to their hunting and fishing.

Generally each Chippewa band roamed over a large territory the use of which belonged to the band. For instance, a band of 600 Chippewas inland of the north shore of Lake Superior might have had thirty large family groups of about 20 persons each. Such a family group might have consisted of a man and his younger brothers, his father and mother, his wives, his younger brothers' wives, and their children. Such a band would have used an area of at least 1,200 square miles and probably much more.

In autumn the band separated into family units and each unit hunted in a separate portion of the band territory. Animals hunted included moose, woodland caribou, bear, beaver, mink, otter, muskrat, porcupine, rabbits, deer, wolf, fox, marten, fisher, and wolverine. The animals were killed with bows and arrows and spears or taken in traps and snares. In the winter of 1670–71 a band of Chippewa on Manitoulin Island in northern Lake Huron took 2,400 moose, using only snares.

In summer the family units joined with others, usually at some good fishing place. Many kinds of fish were caught with hooks, spears, and nets, but the most important were whitefish and sturgeon. Inland from the north shore of Lake Superior, berries were gathered in late summer, and wild rice, which grew in abundance around suitable lakes and marshes, was collected in great quantities.

At certain places, particularly the rapids at Sault Ste Marie, the fish were so abundant that a band could live on fish the year round. The method of catching whitefish in these rapids was highly specialized and required considerable skill.

The fish were taken in baglike nets held in a large wooden fork at the end of a pole 15 feet long. The fisherman stood in the bow of his birchbark canoe as it slid backward over the turbulent rapids. Each thrust of the net gained six or seven large fish and the operation was continued until the canoe was loaded with fish.

These fish-eaters dwelling at the rapids of the St. Mary's River also had some corn that they received in trade from more southerly dwelling Chippewa or Ottawa, who either raised the corn themselves or obtained it in trade from the Huron.

The Chippewa living south of Lake Superior raised some corn, but farming was definitely less important than hunting and fishing. These Chippewa planted their corn in June, then departed from their fields and spent the summer collecting birchbark for canoe manufacture and house coverings, and collecting berries. They also hunted and fished. Fishing in general, and particularly the spearing of sturgeon, was an important summer activity. Sturgeon were taken by harpoon, a long spear with a detachable head or point of bone that was barbed on one side and fastened to a strong line by which the fish were caught after being harpooned.

In late summer when the corn was ripe, these Chippewa returned to planting places for the harvest. The corn often was picked green, as the climate usually did not permit it to ripen. In some years the corn crop failed completely. These Indians also harvested wild rice and planted about one-third of their harvest to insure or increase the supply of wild rice for the following year. After 1730 some of these part-time farming bands of Chippewa concentrated on wild rice, which became as important or more so than corn. This was a transfer of part-time farming activities from corn to wild rice and for these Indians the summer gathering place for the band became the wild rice marshes.

Whether corn or wild rice was the main crop, these Chippewa bands were most dependent upon hunting and fishing for their subsistence; thus after the harvest they again separated into family units and departed for their winter hunting grounds, where they remained until spring.

An important spring activity for some Chippewa bands was the collection of sap from the maple tree and the making of maple sugar. Family units, sometimes several family units, camped at a grove of sugar maples. The trees

Fig. 64.—Chippewa wigwam covered with rolls of birchbark

were tapped and the sap collected in buckets of birchbark was then stored in mooseskin vats of one-hundred-gallon capacity. The women collected the sap and boiled it to make sugar, while the men cut the firewood and hunted.

The Chippewa, being essentially nomadic, had houses that were easily constructed. They lived in oval wigwams that were dome-shaped, made of saplings covered with strips of birchbark (Fig. 64). These strips, more than 20 feet long and about 3 feet wide, were carried in rolls from one camp site to another. The women built the houses, and a house 14 by 20 feet, comfortably housing eight persons could be constructed and ready for occupancy in less than one day.

Travel was by foot or by birchbark canoe. Chippewa canoes were excellent craft and capable of making long voyages even in the open waters of the Upper Great Lakes. In winter travel was on snowshoe. Burdens were transported on one's back, or in winter on a toboggan, and the rest of the year by canoe.

Weapons of the Chippewa were bows and arrows, spears, and clubs. They also had rawhide shields and made some use of armor constructed of wooden

Fig. 65.—Fragments of Chippewa pottery, an arrowhead of chipped flint, and a piece cut from a brass kettle.

rods. Tools included knives and scrapers of chipped flint, bone needles and awls, flint drills, ungrooved axes of stone, fleshing tools of bone, and wooden fire drills.

Among the ordinary utensils were ladles and bowls of wood, containers made of bark, and large and small pottery vessels with open mouths, flaring rims, and round bottoms. These vessels made of fired clay tempered with particles of granitic stone were covered with the imprints of cord-wrapped paddles (Fig. 65).

The social and political organization of the Chippewa was much less elaborate than that of the Huron. Although there were clan and band chiefs, they held relatively little power. There was no political leader for the whole Chippewa tribe, but there was a tribal unity of sorts based upon ties of common language, kinship, and clan membership. These ties cut across bands, helping to unify the bands into a tribal whole.

The kinship system and the social organization based on patrilineal clans were essentially the same as those of the Ottawa and Potawatomi, which are described in the following chapter. Among the clans of the Chippewa were the Crane, Loon, Hawk, Goose, Gull, Catfish, Pike, Sucker, Sturgeon, Whitefish, Merman, Otter, Marten, Moose, Bear, Beaver, Caribou, Wolf, Lynx, and Snake. Members of these clans considered themselves to be in a special relationship of a religious nature with the animal for which the clan was named. Clan symbols were painted or engraved upon various objects. Clan membership was inherited through the male line. Children belonged to the clan of their father and, since marriage within the same clan was prohibited, the mother was always a member of a different clan. This is just the reverse of the matrilineal clan system of the Huron.

The religion of the Chippewa was similar to that of the Ottawa and Potawatomi. The Chippewa, however, probably placed more emphasis upon hunting charms, dreams about success in hunting, and methods of divination. Like other northern Algonkian peoples, the Chippewa treated the bear with special respect and held ceremonies after a bear was killed.

There was no special priesthood, but shamans, or medicine men, attempted to control the good and evil power permeating the natural world in which the Chippewa lived. The most highly organized portion of Chippewa religious life revolved around a Feast of the Dead somewhat similar to that of the Huron and the Midewiwin, or Grand Medicine Society.

The Grand Medicine Society was an organization devoted to healing the sick by religious means. The Society was divided into four grades or degrees taken in succession. Each degree required various ritual acts and a large payment. A Mide of the fourth degree was believed to possess great supernatural power. Admission to membership in the Society was by dedication of a child at birth or by application. One might dream that he should join the Medicine Society. Applicants accepted by the Society were assigned to members for instructions in healing and religious ceremonies. Parts of the instructions and some ritual songs were recorded by means of pictures painted or incised on birchbark. This was not true writing, as each picture or unit of a picture merely suggested the idea that was meant to be recorded.

The Chippewa, better than any other tribe in the Upper Great Lakes region, survived the impact of the white man's civilization, diseases, and wars. This was because they occupied lands least suitable for farming and were remote from the white settlements. For many years the Chippewa engaged in hunting and trapping for the fur trade and some are still doing it today. Although Chippewa tribal culture as described here has changed greatly, there are still many hundreds of these Indians living in the northern parts of the Upper Great Lakes region.

REFERENCES | FENTON, 1940; KIDD, 1952; KINIETZ, 1940; LONG, 1791; MOONEY and THOMAS, 1912a; POPHAM, 1950; QUIMBY, 1958c; RIDLEY, 1952a, 1952b, 1954.

13. THE OTTAWA AND THE POTAWATOMI

A.D. 1600–1760

The Ottawa and the Potawatomi were culturally similar. At about A.D. 1600 the several bands of the Ottawa occupied areas in northeastern Michigan and Ontario bordering on Lake Huron and the Potawatomi probably were dwelling in western Michigan. By 1634 the Potawatomi had moved to the opposite side of Lake Michigan and were living in northeastern Wisconsin. By 1700 they were expanding southward along the Wisconsin shore of Lake Michigan and soon became the dominant tribe in the Chicago area and southern Michigan.

After 1650 the Ottawa moved westward to escape the Iroquois. The Ottawa first settled near Green Bay and then moved to the upper peninsula of Michigan and by 1750 into the upper half of the lower peninsula of Michigan.

The Ottawa were divided into four large bands, the Kiskakons, the Sinago, the Ottawa of Sable, and the Nassauketon, or People of the Fork. The Potawatomi too were divided into bands at this period but their names are not known.

The Ottawa and the Potawatomi were semisedentary. In summer they lived in villages and were agricultural. In autumn they separated into family groups and departed for their winter hunting grounds, where they remained until spring.

They hunted deer, elk, bear, beaver, muskrats, and probably all of the other available animals, by means of bows and arrows, spears, snares, and traps. Fishing was important too. Fish were caught with hook and line, nets, and spears. Hunting and fishing were male occupations, whereas planting of crops and harvesting was done by the women. Digging sticks and wooden hoes were the only agricultural implements. The women also collected wild vegetal foods such as nuts, roots, berries, and wild rice. Both men and women, at least in later times, collected the sap from maple trees and converted it into sugar. Equipment used consisted of wedges, wooden troughs, birchbark buckets, wooden vessels, and probably pottery.

The villages of the Ottawa and Potawatomi were occupied primarily in the summertime. Dwellings were dome-shaped wigwams made of saplings covered with mats and large bark-covered houses similar to those of the Huron. Some villages were protected by circular palisades of upright logs. Ottawa and Potawatomi villages, unlike those of the Hurons, were located along waterways navigable by canoes. The dome-shaped wigwams were used not only in the villages but also in the winter hunting grounds.

Household furnishings and utensils included woven mats, which when spread on the floor served as chairs and when spread on wooden platforms served as beds; big wooden mortars and pestles for pounding corn into meal; woven bags; baskets; boxes or trunks of rawhide; wooden bowls and ladles; and pottery jars.

Ottawa and Potawatomi pottery like that of the Chippewa was made of clay tempered with particles of granitic stone. Long-bodied jars with round or semipointed bottoms and flaring rims were covered by imprints of cord-wrapped paddles on their exterior surfaces.

Tools included knives and scrapers of chipped flint, awls and needles of bone, drills of chipped flint, fleshing tools of bone, bow drills for making fire by friction, and weaving implements of bone.

Tobacco pipes were elbow forms of clay and stone.

Musical instruments were drums, rattles, flutes, and whistles.

Travel and transportation varied with the seasons. For winter travel there were snowshoes and toboggans. During the rest of the year canoes of birchbark were employed.

The Ottawa and the Potawatomi made their clothing of tanned animal skins and furs. Both sexes wore moccasins of skin. Men wore leggings, garters, breech cloths, belts, shirts, and hats or roaches, or feathers. Women wore leggings, skirts, and shirts. Both sexes used fur robes some of which were woven of strips of rabbit fur. Clothing originally was decorated by painted designs or embroidery with dyed porcupine quills or dyed moose hair. Later, glass beads were used for the decoration of clothing.

Among Ottawa and Potawatomi games lacrosse was probably the most important. Other games were snow snake, the women's game, cup and pin, hoop and dart, dice and bowl, cat's cradle, archery contests, and the game of straws.

The Ottawa and the Potawatomi tribes were subdivided into a number of bands that possessed their own territories and were politically independent of one another, although closely connected by ties of clan, kinship, and language.

A clan was a group of actual and assumed blood relatives, tracing their descent from a hypothetical, single ancestor through the male line. Every tribal member belonged to a clan. One could not marry a member of the same clan, thus in any given family a father and his children belonged to one clan—the mother to another clan. And since these different clans were distributed among all the bands, they gave each tribe a certain unity because fellow clansmen recognized one another as close relatives even when they belonged to different bands.

Among the Potawatomi clans were the following: Carp, Sturgeon, Frog, Crayfish, Turtle, Eagle, Crane, Crow or Raven, Turkey, Blackhawk, Loon, Bald Eagle, Bear, Beaver, Wolf, Elk, Rabbit, Fox, and Thunder.

Ottawa clans included Sturgeon, Turtle, Swan, Eagle, Crane, Crow or Raven, Owl, Bear, Beaver, Wolf, Elk, Moose, Wildcat, Rabbit, Otter, Mink, Thunder, and Moon.

Ties of kinship were additional factors in uniting bands into tribal units among the Ottawa and Potawatomi. Unlike the European-American system, which tends to isolate specific relationships, these tribes possessed a classificatory system that tended to separate generations and to keep together in one category relatives who were kept separate in the European-American system. For instance, the father, all of father's brothers, and the husbands of mother's sisters were called father or stepfather. Similarly mother, all of mother's sisters, and all of the wives of father's brothers were called mother or stepmother.

Grandfathers and all of their brothers were called grandfather, and grandmothers and all of their sisters were called grandmother.

Brothers and sisters were the children of everyone called father and mother. Thus brothers and sisters were the children of relatives we call mother and father, paternal uncles and their wives, and maternal aunts and their husbands.

The family was an extended kin group of male lineage. An average family might consist of a father and mother, father's unmarried sisters and brothers, perhaps some grandparents, and a number of children.

In terms of the reckoning of this kind of kinship, a given male child would have mothers and fathers in other households and bands as well as brothers and sisters in other households and bands. In a population of 400, the size of a given group of kindred might well range from 50 to 100 persons contained within a dozen extended families.

In addition to the close ties of kinship and family, there were numerous affinal relatives obtained by intermarriage between families belonging to dif-

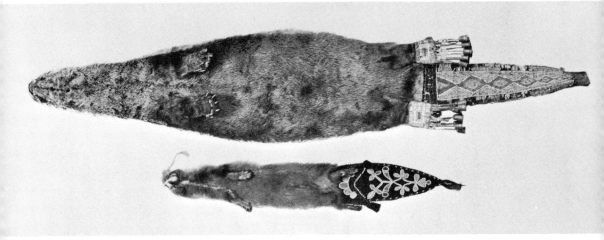

Fig. 66.—Medicine bags of the Potawatomi

ferent clans and even different tribes. Polygamy (polygyny) was common, at least in the period before 1800. Therefore a man could have two or more wives, and although in many instances these wives might have been sisters, in some instances they were not. Thus, in the instances of plural wives who were not sisters, the husband and his relatives would have acquired a larger number of affinal relatives than is possible under the European-American system of marriage.

The religion of the Ottawa and the Potawatomi consisted of an organized body of beliefs and ritual practices involving a concept of a "Great Spirit," deities of fire, sun, and sea, as well as gods of the four directions; manitos, or supernatural power in natural objects, such as rocks, plants, and animals; and personal manitos, or guardians, who were acquired by an individual through fasting and dreaming. It was believed that the human body had but one soul or spirit, which at death followed a trail over the Milky Way to the west, where there was a heaven.

One of the religious organizations of the Ottawa and the Potawatomi was the Midewiwin, or Grand Medicine Society, which functioned to heal the sick and to prolong life. Less important were cults composed of members having a common vision or dream.

The power of the deities and manitos was visualized by the sacred clan bundles; Medicine Society bundles, medicine bags (Fig. 66), and other sacred objects or charms, as well as by rituals and ceremonies which involved dancing to the music of drums, rattles, and whistles and the eating of dogs especially raised for ceremonial feasts. A large body of mythology also served to make real the power of the deities and manitos.

The dead were buried with ceremony, sometimes after having been placed on a scaffold for an indefinite period.

Persons associated by clan membership with the Hare deity were cremated at death.

The aboriginal culture of the Ottawa and the Potawatomi fell apart from the impact of the white man's civilization. Cultural change initiated at the beginning of contact with fur traders and missionaries rapidly accelerated with actual settlement of the Upper Great Lakes region by white men. Involvement in white men's wars and diseases introduced by white men took heavy toll among the tribes. Finally, many of the Ottawa and Potawatomi were removed from the region to new lands west of the Mississippi. However, a few remnants remained and are still living in the Upper Great Lakes region in Michigan, Wisconsin, and Ontario.

REFERENCES | KINIETZ, 1940; MICHELSON, 1911; MOONEY and HEWITT, 1912a, 1912b; QUIMBY, 1940; RITZENTHALER, 1953.

14. THE SAUK, FOX, AND MIAMI

A.D. 1650–1760

Indians of the Sauk, Fox, and Miami tribes lived in the western and southern parts of the Lake Michigan basin of the Upper Great Lakes region. The Sauk and the Fox were in the northern portion of eastern Wisconsin's deciduous forest zone. The Miami lived in southeastern Wisconsin, northeastern Illinois, northwestern Indiana, and southwestern Michigan, a habitat composed of deciduous forest and tall-grass prairie.

By 1700 these tribal locations had shifted in response to pressures of war and the development of the fur trade with Europeans. Some parts of all of these tribes moved southward into portions of Wisconsin, Illinois, and Indiana that were outside of the Upper Great Lakes region, although other parts of the same tribes remained within the region.

The Sauk, Fox, and Miami lived in permanent villages which they occupied in the summer and which they left in the winter to hunt buffalo on the prairies.

Subsistence was based upon a combination of farming and hunting. In cleared fields near the villages the women planted and cultivated corn, beans, and squash with the aid of digging sticks and hoes of wood, shell, or bone. Just before planting, the fields were cleared of the dried cornstalks of the previous crop by burning.

The women protected the corn crop from birds and also did the harvesting. The women also harvested wild rice (*Zizania aquatica*) which grew in suitable places throughout the region and they collected acorns, too. About five bushels of corn and five bushels of wild rice were considered an adequate year's supply for one family. Surplus grain was stored in underground pits lined with bark.

Sometime after the harvest, entire villages moved into the prairies and prairie transition zones for the winter buffalo hunt. This was a communal affair and the villages were deserted except for men and women too old to walk such a distance. Able-bodied men and women, as well as children, walked to the winter hunting grounds. The hunting party was kept together by guards in order to prevent unfair hunting advantages by individuals or small groups.

A common method of killing buffaloes was to surround the herd with a ring of fire by igniting the dry prairie grass. An unfired opening was left in the ring and as the buffalo stampeded through this opening they were shot down with bows and arrows. Using this method a band of Indians could kill as many as 200 buffaloes in one day. The animals thus obtained were divided among the individual families. The buffalo meat was dried by sun or fire and could be preserved for more than four months.

At other times of the year elk, deer, bear, and beaver were killed in the forests by small parties of hunters on relatively short trips from their villages. Twelve animals per day might be taken by a good hunter. A French visitor at one of the Miami villages in 1702 wrote that "it was a real pleasure to see the Miami occasionally bringing into their village some enormous bears, tamed in the course of their hunting, and driven before them with switches, like sheep to the slaughter house."

The villages of the Sauk, Fox, and Miami consisted of clusters of elongated wigwams (Fig. 67). These were made of saplings inserted in the ground and bent over and tied together in the middle of the house to form a dome-like roof. Over this framework were tied many mats woven of prepared rushes. In each village there was a council house, larger than the others, but otherwise similar. Some villages were fortified by means of log palisades. The villages were usually occupied from the end of April to October, the warmer half of the year. The remaining time was spent in temporary encampments during the winter hunt.

The Sauk, Fox, and Miami usually traveled from one place to another on foot. The women carried the burdens on their backs by means of headbands and packstraps. There was some use of dugout canoes, but by and large these tribes of Indians were not canoe people. The Sauk and Fox learned the use of birchbark canoes, snowshoes, and the toboggan from northern Great Lakes tribes, such as Ottawa and Chippewa, and made some use of them after their culture had changed in response to pressures of the fur trade. But only the wooden dugout canoe is typical of their original tribal culture.

The clothing of the Sauk, Fox, and Miami was similar. In the summertime

Fig. 67.—Mat-covered wigwam of type used by Sauk, Fox, and Miami

men wore moccasins and breechcloths. In winter they added shirts and leggings made of deer or elk skin and buffalo skin robes with the fur left on.

In winter the women wore moccasins, leggings, and dresses of elk and deerskin and sometimes an outer skirt of cloth or skin. They also used robes of buffalo skin. Summer clothing probably consisted only of moccasins and some kind of skirt.

Robes were sometimes ornamented with painted designs or with porcupine-quill embroidery in red and white.

Women generally wore their hair long and gathered at the neck, whereas men had a variety of styles. Men had their bodies and faces painted in various ways and sometimes tattooed.

The political organization of the Sauk, Fox, and Miami was similar to that of the Ottawa and Potawatomi. The largest political unit was the band. The Miami, for instance, were divided into six large bands, two of which, the Wea and Piankashaw, later came to be recognized as separate tribes. There was no tribal chief, but there were band or village chiefs and clan chiefs. Village and band affairs were handled by councils of clan chiefs and tribal affairs were the concern of a council of band and village chiefs. Tribal unity, however, was not achieved by political organization but through the ties of language, clan, and kinship.

The kinship system of the Sauk, Fox, and Miami was different from the European-American system of classifying relatives used in modern America. It was also different from that of the Chippewa, Ottawa, and Potawatomi.

Whereas the Chippewa, Ottawa, and Potawatomi system tended to separate generations, the Sauk, Fox, and Miami kinship terminology ignored generations. It stressed lineage in unilateral descent in the male line through one's mother's brother. Mother's brother was an uncle and his male descendants through males were uncles. The daughters of these uncles were called mothers and their children were one's brothers and sisters.

This confusion of generation was especially perplexing to European explorers who thought the Indians were lying about relationships. One Frenchman (at about A.D. 1700) wrote, "All call each other relatives—I have seen men of eighty claim that young girls were their mothers." Such a claim was, of course, valid, when one understands the kinship system of the Sauk, Fox, and Miami, which was also typical of neighboring tribes on the south and west.

The perpetuation of uncle and mother terms through the mother's brother is a way of perpetuating the male family line of one's mother and of recognizing the importance of this male lineage. Such recognition implies considerations of wealth and prestige which could only develop with a relatively abundant supply of food and a sedentary life. This in turn reflects the milder and richer environment of the Sauk, Fox, and Miami when contrasted with that of the Chippewa.

Patrilineal clans divided groups of kin and extended kinlike relationships to other members of the clan. A child belonged to the clan of his father. Thus a boy and his mother belonged to different clans, and so the male lineage of his mother's brother was of a clan different from his own. One could not marry within the clan, thus all marriages were between persons of different clans. Clan members thought they were descended from a mythical founder with supernatural powers who took the form of an animal.

The clans of the Sauk tribe included the Deer, Bear, Panther, Wolf, Swan, Bald Eagle, Perch, Bass, and Sturgeon. Among the clans of the Fox tribe were the Bear, Wolf, Fox, Elk, Swan, Partridge, and Bass. The Miami clans included the Bear, Deer, Elk, Crane, and Acorn.

The division of labor among the Sauk, Fox, and Miami was similar to that of most of the tribes in the Upper Great Lakes region. The women worked in the fields; transported burdens; made clothing; took care of chil-

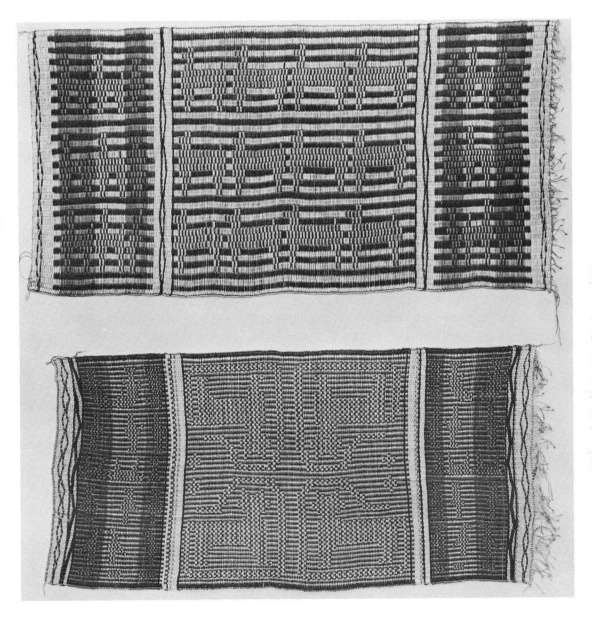

Fig. 68.—*Woven mats of the Sauk and Fox Indians. Design on* UPPER *mat represents deer; design on* LOWER *mat represents group of mythical long-tailed underwater panthers.*

dren; wove mats (Fig. 68), baskets, and cloth; made pottery; did the cooking; and engaged in many other activities. Men cleared land for fields; made tools, weapons, and some utensils; engaged in warfare; did the hunting; made dugout canoes; and were the major participants in political and religious activities.

Weapons included wooden clubs, spears, and bows and arrows. Spears and arrows were tipped with points of chipped flint. Among the tools were wooden drills for making fire by friction, knives and scrapers of chipped flint, awls and needles of bone, flint drills, bone weaving-tools, and ungrooved axes of ground and polished stone. Utensils included large wooden mortars and pestles for pounding corn into flour, pottery vessels, wooden bowls and ladles, spoons and ladles made of mussel shells, and rawhide containers.

Cloth was woven of spun buffalo hair and dyed black, yellow, or deep red. Bags were also woven of spun buffalo hair and plant fiber.

Musical instruments consisted of drums, various kinds of rattles, flutes and whistles, and the musical rasp, a notched stick or bone that produced sound when a stick or similar object was rubbed across the notches.

Ornaments used by the Sauk, Fox, and Miami were beads and pendants of shell, and feathers or tufts of down used in various ways.

Tobacco was used for pleasure as well as for ceremonial purposes. It was smoked in elbow-shaped pipes of stone or clay to which were added stems of reed or wood.

Little information is available on the religious beliefs of the Sauk, Fox, and Miami in the period before tribal cultures were changed by contact with white men's civilization. There seems to have been a number of deities, supreme among which was the sun, maker of all things and master of life. There was also a belief in manito, the power for good or evil that existed in all things, animate or inanimate, but this was not manifested to the same degree that it was among the Ottawa and Potawatomi, and particularly the Chippewa.

The Midewiwin, or Grand Medicine Society, was an important religious feature of the tribal culture of Sauk, Fox, and Miami. Members of the society were believed to be able to heal the sick and to maintain tribal well-being by supernatural means. There were four degrees of membership based upon an ascending order of complexity, skill, and prestige. Healing rites were also performed by lesser medicine men, or shamans, who were not members of the Midewiwin.

The Grand Medicine Society, clans, war parties, and certain individuals or families possessed sacred medicine bundles—collections of magical paraphernalia held in woven bags or bags made of mink or otter skins and wrapped in small woven mats made especially for that purpose. Among the contents of medicine bags were quartz crystals, fossils, shells, clusters of bird feathers, skins of special birds, effigy carvings, and all sorts of charms and amulets. On many different occasions there were religious rituals and ceremonies involving the use of the sacred bundles.

The Sauk, Fox, and Miami buried their dead in shallow graves lined with bark or with a section of an old dugout canoe. Corpses were arrayed in their clothing, faces and hair were colored with mineral pigments, and they were accompanied by tools, weapons, utensils, ornaments, food, and tobacco. The bodies were placed in an extended or sitting position in the grave. After the grave was covered with earth a double lean-to of small logs was erected over it. In some instances, bodies were placed on scaffolds or in trees and subsequently buried.

REFERENCES   BLAIR, 1911; HEWITT, 1912; KINIETZ, 1940; MOONEY and THOMAS, 1912*b*; TAX, 1937.

15. THE WINNEBAGO AND THE MENOMINI

A.D. 1600–1760

THE WINNEBAGO

The Winnebago Indians lived in northeastern Wisconsin in the area embracing Lake Winnebago, the city of Green Bay, and the southern part of the Door Peninsula. This was Winnebago territory at the time of the arrival of the first Europeans, and archeological evidence indicates that the ancestors of the Winnebago had lived there for many hundreds of years.

Although the Winnebago language indicated ties with Chiwere Siouan groups, the tribal culture was essentially similar to that of the Sauk, Fox, and Miami. The Winnebago made their living by farming and hunting and lived in permanent villages.

They raised corn, squash, beans, and tobacco, and collected wild rice, acorns and other nuts, and berries. After the crops were harvested, the Winnebago went on a communal buffalo hunt into the prairies to the southwest of their permanent villages, outside of the Upper Great Lakes region.

Winnebago houses were dome-shaped wigwams like those of the Sauk, Fox, and Miami. They were 12 to 40 feet in length, 10 to 20 feet wide, and about 15 feet high, made of saplings and covered with woven mats.

Most tools, utensils, and weapons of the historic Winnebago were the same as those of the prehistoric or ancestral Winnebago described in chapter x as the Lake Winnebago culture. As indicated there, the pottery was unique in style and suggestive of Siouan groups in the Upper Mississippi Valley. This style of pottery persisted into the historic period and was an integral part of Winnebago tribal culture, which in most other respects was like that of Miami, Fox, and Sauk.

Winnebago social organization also was like that of the Sauk, Fox, Miami, and Menomini, with a kinship system that stressed lineage in unilateral descent in the male line through one's mother's brother. Some details of this type of system have been presented in chapter xiv.

140

Like other Indians in the Upper Great Lakes region, the Winnebago were divided into clans. Each person was born into the clan of his father. One could neither marry someone of his own clan nor marry into other clans of the same division. He had to marry someone in a clan belonging to another division.

Among the Winnebago, in later times at least, there were two divisions, the Upper or Air phratry and the Lower or Earth phratry. The Upper or Air division consisted of the Thunderbird clan, the War clan, the Eagle clan, and the Pigeon clan. The Lower or Earth division consisted of the Bear, Wolf, Water-Spirit, Deer, Elk, Buffalo, Fish, and Snake clans. Clans present among the Winnebago in 1736 but extinct by the late nineteenth century were Lynx and Skunk. The Thunderbird was the leading clan of the Upper division and the Bear was the leading clan of the Lower division.

Civil authority was in the hands of the Thunderbird clan. Chieftainship of the principal Winnebago village and perhaps of the tribe seems to have been hereditary within this clan. The lodge of the Thunderbird clan was the peace lodge presided over by the village civil chief. Disputes between the Indians were adjudicated there. There was also the right of asylum in this lodge. War chieftainship seems to have been hereditary within the Bear clan, which was in charge of war and police activities. The lodge of the Bear clan was the place of execution and other punishment. This clan also was in charge of policing the annual buffalo hunt, which was a communal affair.

Each clan possessed a sacred bundle. A sacred bundle consisted of a number of objects, such as feathers, rock crystals, fossils, figurines, special pipes, charms, amulets, and other things believed to contain great supernatural power. These objects, placed in skin or woven bags, were made into a bundle that was wrapped in hides or matting.

The religious concepts of the Winnebago were much like those of Sauk, Fox, and Miami. Their principal supernatural beings appear in sacred stories, such as that of the Earthmaker, who sent out The Trickster, The Bladder, The Turtle, He Who Wears Heads as Earrings, and The Hare to rid the world of evil spirits and giants, so that it would be a good place for the Winnebago to live. Some other Winnebago deities were Sun, Moon, Morning Star, Earth, Water, Night Spirits, and Disease Giver. The Winnebago, like the other Upper Great Lakes Indians, had the concept of manito-supernatural power, good or evil, present in the inanimate as well as animate aspects of nature.

The Winnebago had a grand medicine society similar to the Midewiwin of other Upper Great Lakes tribes. Its function was to heal the sick, prolong life, and instil Winnebago virtues among the people of the tribe. Although it was a secret society, men and women could become members by payment of a fee. The membership of the society was divided among five ceremonial bands responsible for specific parts of the rituals. The annual major ceremony of this society was held during the summer.

A major ceremony held in winter by the Winnebago tribe was the Winter Feast. Its function was to increase the tribal war and hunting powers by propitiating all of the deities with offerings of food and deerskins. In spring there was the Buffalo Dance, a ceremony for the magical calling of the buffalo herds. Winnebago religious ideas and rituals not only explained the world about them to the Indians, but also helped them to obtain food, shelter, and clothing, and to maintain health; and contributed to tribal well-being.

The clothing of the Winnebago was similar to that of the Sauk, Fox, and Miami. So was the Winnebago mode of travel and transportation. They either walked from one place to another or used wooden dugout canoes.

At death the Winnebago souls were believed to journey to a soul world. To help the souls on this journey various useful things, food, tools, utensils, weapons, and ornaments, were placed in the graves with the deceased. The bodies, dressed in their finery, were wrapped in bark, mats, or skins and placed in shallow graves in an extended position.

Winnebago tribal culture changed in response to the demands of the fur trade with white men. In the nineteenth century many of the Winnebago moved westward into the prairies and plains, but some remained in their old homeland and their descendants are still living in northeastern Wisconsin.

THE MENOMINI

The Menomini lived along the Menominee River, that now is the boundary between Wisconsin and the upper peninsula of Michigan. Their principal village was at the mouth of this river, where it enters Green Bay. The Menomini occupied this area from prior to 1634 until after 1760.

The Menomini spoke a distinct dialect of the Algonkian family of languages more closely related to Sauk and Fox than to Chippewa or Potawatomi. Yet the closest tribal relations were between the Menomini and their Siouan-speaking neighbors, the Winnebago.

In general, Menomini tribal culture was much like that of the Winnebago. The Menomini kinship system, social structure, and political organization were essentially like those of the Winnebago. Menomini religious concepts and practices were like those of the Winnebago. And much of Menomini material culture, including the use of wooden dugout canoes, was like that of the Winnebago. The essential cultural difference seems to have been in subsistence. The Menomini probably utilized wild rice to a greater degree than the Winnebago or other Upper Great Lakes tribes.

The Menomini made their living by farming, harvesting wild rice (*Zizania aquatica*), hunting, fishing, and collecting nuts, roots, and berries. They cultivated corn, squash, beans, and tobacco, but apparently to a more limited extent than the Winnebago. On the other hand, they harvested the wild rice, that grew abundantly in their environment and seem to have been most dependent upon it as a vegetal crop.

Although the Menomini did not deliberately sow wild rice as did some of the Chippewa, they did in fact sow it because it was impossible to harvest the wild rice without accidentally losing at least 50 per cent of the seeds in the water. Thus, by the very act of harvesting one year's crop of wild rice, the Menomini were helping to sow the next year's crop. This is in keeping with a later Menomini statement that, "Whenever the Menomini enter a region the wild rice spreads ahead, whenever they leave it the wild rice passes."

The wild rice grows in shallow, slowly running waters with mud bottoms. When the wild rice had ripened sufficiently, the Menomini in their dugout canoes tied stalks of rice together and bent them over. Then when the grain was fully ripe, the canoes were poled down the open water aisles and the clusters of bent-over stalks of grain were beaten with sticks and the individual grains fell into the dugout canoe. Sometimes the rice was harvested directly into the canoe without preliminary typing of groups of stalks.

The dried grain was beaten in special bags to separate the seeds from the husks. It could be prepared for eating in many different ways, but boiling was most commonly used. A popular dish was boiled wild rice and maple sugar.

In addition to wild rice and cultivated crops, there were gathered vegetal foods that included fruits and berries, acorns and other nuts, and various roots.

Fishing, particularly for sturgeon, was an important economic activity. Fish were taken with barbed spears, hooks, and nets.

Hunting does not seem to have been as important as sturgeon-fishing or the harvesting of wild rice. The hunting of buffalo in the prairies was a communal affair, whereas the hunting of forest animals was undertaken by lone hunters or small groups.

The Menomini lived in sedentary villages. There was one main village near the mouth of the Menominee River, where it flows into Green Bay, and several subsidiary settlements in the vicinity. Houses, like those of the Winnebago, Sauk, Fox, and Miami, were dome-shaped, made of sapling frames covered with woven mats.

The Menomini were excellent weavers. They made fine mats and wove excellent twined bags of twisted vegetal fiber alone, or of twisted vegetal fiber and spun buffalo hair (Fig. 69). Some of these bags were decorated with geometric designs and figures of humans or animals woven into them with dyed cords. The Winnebago, Sauk, Fox, and Miami made similar bags and mats.

Like all of the other tribes in the Upper Great Lakes region, the Menomini divided their year into twelve lunar months. The Menomini calendar was as follows:

January	Great god moon
February	Sucker moon
March	Snow crust moon
April	Sugar-making moon
May	Loose-bark moon
June	Strawberry moon
July	Blueberry moon
August	Great ripening moon
September	Turning leaves moon
October	Falling leaves moon
November	Frozen-ground moon
December	God moon

The Menomini and the Winnebago, even though they spoke radically different languages, lived at peace with one another in adjoining areas. It is likely that the Menomini was the weaker of the two tribes. It is probable

Fig. 69.—Woven bag of the Menomini Indians

that the Menomini and the Winnebago had close economic ties. For instance, it would not be surprising to learn that the Winnebago traded surplus corn, squashes, and tobacco to the Menomini in exchange for surplus wild rice, fish, and skins of northern forest animals.

With the development of the fur trade in the Upper Great Lakes region Menomini culture changed. The aboriginal social organization based on sedentary village and dual division of the tribe shifted to a mobile-band organization. And, like other Upper Great Lakes tribes, the Menomini became "specialized laborers in a great outdoor fur factory." But, although the Menomini aboriginal culture for the most part had disappeared by A.D. 1800, the Menomini retained their tribal identity into the twentieth century and Menomini Indians today are to be found in Wisconsin not far from their aboriginal homeland.

REFERENCES | DORSEY and RADIN, 1912; HOFFMAN, 1893; KEESING, 1939; KINIETZ, 1940; LAWSON, 1907; MOONEY and THOMAS, 1912c; RADIN, 1923.

16. THE BREAKDOWN OF
TRIBAL CULTURE
A.D. 1760–1820

By 1760 there had arisen in the Upper Great Lakes region a uniformity of tribal culture brought about by contact with white men and the change in native economic systems caused by the fur trade.

The tribal cultures as they were before prolonged contact with Europeans have been described in previous chapters. They were adapted to various habitats which they exploited to obtain their food, shelter, clothing, tools, weapons, and utensils.

However, by 1760 every Indian in the region was in some way dependent upon the fur trade and thus in a sense was working for the white men. Animal skins, particularly those of beaver, had become money. And the Indians had to obtain this animal-skin money in order to buy the tools, weapons, utensils, clothing, ornaments, and even food that they formerly had produced themselves.

As the Indians became dependent upon the fur trade they shifted their tribal locations. Tribes tended to congregate along the trading routes and to establish their hunting grounds in relation to fur-trading centers. The tribes also engaged in warfare over hunting grounds and trading advantages. The nations of the fur traders also fought each other to obtain economic advantages, and the Indians allied with one white nation or another became soldiers of foreign powers.

Remnants of once powerful tribes amalgamated with other tribal remnants. Bands of various tribes established joint villages with bands of other tribes and even large portions of tribes on occasion lived in the same village with other tribes.

The fur trade seems to have most favored the aboriginal mode of life of the Chippewa who lived by hunting and fishing. Consequently, as the Pan-Indian culture developed in response to the fur trade, it developed in the direction of the Chippewa culture type. But with all the Indians con-stantly mixing with one another, acquiring a common material culture based on white men's manufactures and European imports, and changing socially in response to new economic and social conditions as well as wars and introduced diseases, it is no wonder that tribal cultures were reduced to a common level of Pan-Indian culture.

This culture existed in the Upper Great Lakes from some time prior to 1760 to about 1820, when the fur trade was no longer important in the region. The characteristics of this culture were as follows.

The Indians made their living by hunting and trapping animals, par-ticularly beaver, and exchanging the skins with white traders for guns, knives, hatchets, blankets, clothing, ornaments, brass kettles, rum, and a multitude of other items manufactured and used by the contemporary white men in Europe and America. The meat of the animals was used for food, and foods were also purchased from the trader, who usually had a stock of flour, corn, wild rice, and other items. Some Indians still practiced summer farming in suitable locations and raised corn, beans, native and imported squashes, peas, watermelons, imported fruits, and tobacco and other crops, much of which were sold to the traders. Wild rice was also sold to traders.

All of the vegetal products produced by the Indians were utilized by traders, and surpluses were sold back to the Indians.

The Indians used snares, steel traps, and flintlock guns for hunting. For fishing they had nets, iron fishhooks, and barbed spears of bone or iron. They had hoes of iron for cultivating their crops.

In addition to their old-style dwellings, the Indians made use of log cabins and similarly shaped houses covered with bark. Household utensils included brass kettles; pewter and silver spoons; wooden ladles and bowls; various kinds of glass bottles; Chinese blue and white porcelain and later Staffordshire pottery of similar shapes and decoration; glass mirrors; iron strike-a-lights for starting fires; and many other items that were also part of the material culture of the contemporary white men.

Clothing was made of various kinds of imported cloth and often decorated with native designs in colored beads of glass or in silk ribbon appliqué (Figs. 70, 71). Moccasins were still made in the old way but were decorated with glass beads or ribbon appliqué. Imported woolen blankets were used both as clothing and as robes for sleeping.

Ornaments included different kinds of colored glass beads (Fig. 72), shell

*Fig. 70.—Chippewa dress costume similar
to type worn A.D. 1800.*

Fig. 71.—Potawatomi costumes of type worn about A.D. 1800

beads and gorgets manufactured by white men, and ornaments of silver or brass. Silver ornaments were so popular among the Indians that silversmiths in England and North America made silver objects of fine quality especially for the Indian trade. Common types of silver ornaments were crescent-shaped gorgets, round gorgets (Fig. 73), various kinds of brooches, single- and double-barred crosses (Fig. 74), armbands, bracelets, and earbobs. Less common were hair pipes, earwheels, hair plates, animal effigies (Fig. 74), lockets, crowns, hatbands, and cradle-board decorations.

The tools used by the Indians included steel hatchets, various knives, awls, needles, scissors, coiled-spring hair pullers for removing sparse facial and body hair that was unwanted, drills, scraper blades, and chisels.

Tobacco was smoked in white clay pipes manufactured in Europe. These pipes were imported in tremendous quantities.

Other popular objects supplied by the traders were brass bells, jew's-harps, and tinkling cones of brass. The bells and tinkling cones were attached to ceremonial clothing and produced rhythmic sounds when the wearer was walking or dancing.

Much of the material culture of the Upper Great Lakes Indians in the period from about 1760 to 1820 was identical to that of the white men of the period, especially of those who had been peasants or lived on the frontier. Moreover, many of the white men had Indian girls either as slaves or wives and had children by them. But the white men on the frontier were living more like Indians than vice versa, and this was to be expected. The white traders took over the birchbark canoe of the northern Great Lakes and used it throughout the region. They also took over the use of snowshoes where climate warranted. The environment, in fact, was such that the white man of the period had to live much like the Indians or perish.

But despite similarities in material culture between Indians and frontier whites, the Indian was still an Indian. His languages and social customs still survived with considerable strength. The social culture was much more resistant to change than was material culture, although it too was changing.

The traditional lines of social authority were disappearing. The young people were no longer honoring the old ways. And the social culture also had to change in response to new requirements. The Chippewa, for instance, had to add two new clans to their tribal list.

The Chippewa, as was indicated previously, had clans, membership in which was inherited from one's father. Among some bands there arose a

Fig. 72.—Trade beads of colored glass

Fig. 73.—Silver gorgets, ornaments, obtained from fur traders

problem because British and American men, resident among the Indians, had married Chippewa girls and the children were without membership in a clan. The problem was solved in this way. Since the totem of the British must be the lion, because pictures of lions appeared on British medals and seals, all British men were assumed to be members of the Lion clan and their children would be members of the Lion clan. Thus the Chippewa acquired a new clan whose symbol was the African lion and whose members were of British descent. Similarly the American men must belong to the Eagle clan because the eagle, judging from arms and seals, must be the totem or symbol of the Americans. So the Chippewa acquired an American Eagle clan to which belonged the Americans and their children by Chippewa women.

Religious authority too was breaking down, partly because of missionary endeavors, but also because continued violation of religious taboos and rites, first by white men and later by younger Indians, had brought forth no supernatural punishment.

The most demoralizing factor was liquor, which was readily accepted by the Indians, probably at first for religious reasons. The Indians obtained religious experiences from dreams and visions gotten by fasting and fatigue. Rum produced dreams and hallucinations much more quickly than fasting, and rum and drunkenness became a prominent aspect of the fur trade.

Just how demoralizing the rum was is indicated by the following excerpts from the journal of a fur trader among the Indians of the north shore of Lake Superior in 1778: ". . . with the rum we gave them they continued in a state of inebriety three days and nights, during which frolic they killed four of their own party." In another instance, "I traded for their skins and furs and gave them some rum, with which they had a frolic which lasted for three days and nights; on this occasion five men were killed, and one woman dreadfully burned." And finally, "I cannot help relating the method I was obliged to adopt to quiet an old Indian woman . . . I infused forty drops of the tincture of cantharides and the same quantity of laudanum into a glass of rum. . . . I then repeated the dose, which she also drank, and then fell on the floor."

These examples are not unusual. Whole bands of Indians traded their furs for rum and engaged in violent drunkenness. And this in no small measure contributed to their cultural breakdown.

The burial customs among the Upper Great Lakes Indian tribes were

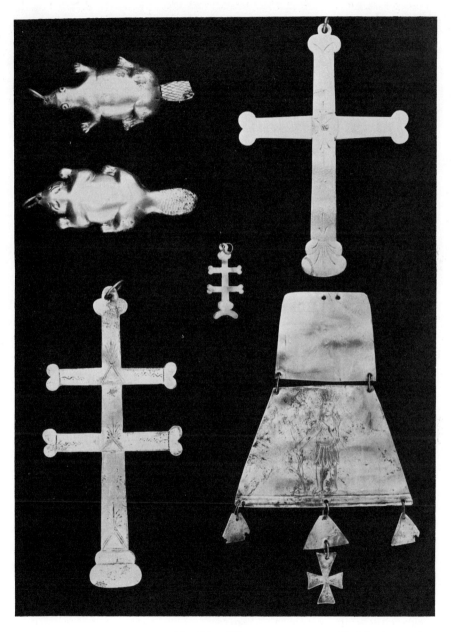

Fig. 74.—Silver ornaments provided by fur traders

Fig. 75.—Alcohol lamp of brass and peppermint bottles of glass

essentially the same in this period. The deceased were placed in graves dug into sandy knolls and ridges or sometimes into old burial mounds of much earlier periods. In rare instances, a low mound was erected over the grave, but generally a small log or pole structure, oblong with a peaked roof, was built over the filled-in grave pit.

The deceased were laid in an extended or flexed position, and tools, weapons, utensils, and ornaments, most of them purchased from traders, were placed in the grave. A man, for instance, would be buried with his loaded flintlock gun; a beaded pouch of bullets; extra gun flints; an iron ax; white clay tobacco pipes made in Scotland; silver armbands, gorgets, and ear ornaments made in London or Montreal; a glass bottle of peppermint oil for his stomach (Fig. 75); a flint and steel (strike-a-light) and punk for starting fires; pewter dishes of food; powdered vermillion face paint; and any other things that might be useful to him in the world of spirits.

An Indian woman might well be buried with her brass kettles; silver brooches; necklaces of colored glass beads; Chinese blue and white porcelain or Staffordshire china from England; an iron ax for chopping wood; a hand mirror; a jew's-harp; and other grave furnishings considered necessary in the spirit world.

The Pan-Indian culture of the Upper Great Lakes region was in part an adjustment to the fur trade of the white men; and when the fur trade ended in the region, the Pan-Indian culture began to disintegrate. The Indian livelihood was almost completely dependent upon the trapping and hunting of fur-bearing animals. As these animals became scarce, the fur traders moved westward. Also white settlers were moving into the Upper Great Lakes region.

The Indians were left without a livelihood. They no longer had the means of purchasing their supplies, and much of their old way of life was lost to them. A great many Indians moved into areas where wild rice could be harvested, some tried farming, others moved westward, and many were left in a rather hopeless condition on the frontier. It was these Indians, deprived of their aboriginal culture and left in a badly depressed economic situation, who made the last futile but bloody attempts to delay white settlement of the Upper Great Lakes region. A cultural continuity that had lasted about 13,000 years was destroyed by the advance of Old World civilization.

REFERENCES | Long, 1791; Michelson, 1911; Quimby, 1937, 1938, 1958d.

GLOSSARY

ALGOMA STAGE. A postglacial stage of the Upper Great Lakes when the water level was 595 or 596 feet above present sea level.

AMULET. An object believed to possess supernatural power.

ANCULOSA. A genus of freshwater snails, the shells of which were made into beads by some Indians.

AQUA-PLANO. A prehistoric type of culture found in the Upper Great Lakes and similar to Plano culture of the western United States.

ARCHAIC. An ancient stage of culture in North America.

ARGILLITE. A slatelike stone.

ARTIFACT. Any object made by humans.

ATLATL. Another name for spear-thrower.

BANNERSTONE. A perforated object of polished stone of any of a variety of forms. They seem to have been used as weights on spear-throwers.

BIRDSTONE. A polished stone object, shaped somewhat like a bird or an animal, with perforations in the base. It seems to have been used with the spear-thrower either as a weight or a handle.

BLUE ISLAND CULTURE. A Late Woodland period culture known from southern Cook County, Illinois.

BOREAL ARCHAIC. The archaic culture of North America that was adapted to the northern forests.

BOWMANVILLE STAGE. Another and less desirable name for the Two Creeks low water stage that preceded the Valders glacial advance.

BROHM-SITE PEOPLE. The Aqua-Plano Indians who lived at the Brohm site, Thunder Bay, Ontario.

CALUMET STAGE. A glacial lake stage in the Lake Michigan basin when the water level was 620 feet above present sea level.

CARBON 14. A radioactive isotope that occurs in the earth's atmosphere.

CEDAR POINT STAGE. A post-Algonquin lake stage with a water level about 493 feet above present sea level.

CELT. An ungrooved ax of stone or metal.

CHIPPEWA INDIANS. A tribe of Indians found in Upper Great Lakes region at time of first arrival of Europeans.

CHIPPEWA-STANLEY STAGE. A post-Algonquin stage of low water levels. The water plane in the Lake Michigan basin was 230 feet above present sea level and that in the Huron basin was 180 feet or less.

CHIWERE SIOUAN INDIANS. Those tribes who spoke dialects of the Chiwere Siouan division of the Siouan language. They include Winnebago, Oto, Iowa, and Missouri tribes of Indians.

CLAN. A unilateral grouping of relatives into a kin group larger than the family.

CLOVIS FLUTED POINT. A type of leaf-shaped spearhead with a longitudinal groove extending from its base toward its tip.

CORD-MARKED POTTERY. Pottery with exterior malleations produced by pressing or stamping the vessel surface with a cord-wrapped paddle-like tool while the clay was still plastic.

CULTURE. As used by archeologists, culture consists of material objects such as tools, weapons, utensils, ornaments, amulets, art, etc., as well as acts, beliefs, attitudes, institutions, customs, rituals, etc. that function in social contexts dependent upon the use of symbols.

DENTATE STAMP. A comblike object or tool with teeth used to impress decorative motifs on pottery vessels while clay was still plastic.

EARLY POSTGLACIAL PERIOD. The time immediately following the disappearance of the glacier in a region. In the Upper Great Lakes this period is from 3000 to 1500 B.C.

EARLY VALDERS RETREAT. The initial stages in the retreat of the Valders glacier. This period lasted from 8500 to 8000 B.C.

EARLY WOODLAND INDIANS. The first Indians in the region who had pottery and/or burial mounds.

EFFIGY MOUND. A mound of earth constructed in the shape of something, such as an animal or a bird.

EFFIGY MOUND INDIANS. The Indians responsible for the effigy mounds and other remnants of Effigy Mound culture in Wisconsin during the Late Woodland period.

FISHER CULTURE. An Indian culture of the Late Woodland period found in the southern part of the Upper Great Lakes region.

FLINT. Any one of a variety of stones that break with a conchoidal fracture and could be shaped by flaking and chipping techniques.

FLUTED POINT. A leaf-shaped point with a longitudinal groove from the base toward the tip.

FOX INDIANS. A tribe of Indians that lived in the Upper Great Lakes region at the time of first exploration by Europeans.

GEOCHRONOLOGY. The arrangement of data and events that relate to the study of the earth in the order of the time of their occurrence.

GLACIAL LAKE. A lake formed in front of a glacier. The glacier acts as a dam holding the lake water between it and the natural barriers of those portions of the lake basin free of glacial ice.

GLENWOOD STAGE. A glacial lake stage in the Lake Michigan basin when the water level was 640 feet above present sea level.

GORGET. An ornament or badge of stone, shell, or metal, perforated for suspension, and worn on the chest.

GRAY TILL DEPOSITS. Unstratified glacial material deposited directly by the ice and consisting of gray clay, sand, gravel, and boulders in varying proportions.

GRIT-TEMPERED POTTERY. Pottery made from clay to which had been added particles of grit, usually minute bits of granitic rock. Such tempering of the clay was supposed to keep the vessel from breaking when it was fired to harden the clay.

HOPEWELL INDIANS. The bearers of a prehistoric culture found in a number of places in the eastern United States during the Middle Woodland period.

HURON INDIANS. A populous tribe of Indians living in the eastern part of the Upper Great Lakes region at the time of arrival of the first Europeans.

IROQUOIS INDIANS. A confederacy of different Indian tribes speaking various dialects of the Iroquoion language family. They lived mostly in the area of the state of New York.

KICKAPOO INDIANS. A tribe of Indians living just west of the Upper Great Lakes region at the time of the arrival of the first Europeans.

KIRKFIELD OUTLET. An extinct channel or outlet of ancient stages of the Upper Great Lakes. It is located near Kirkfield, Ontario, and was part of a drainage way from the Lake Huron basin to the Lake Ontario basin.

KISKAKON. A large band or major division of the Ottawa tribe.

KORAH STAGE. A post-Algonquin stage of the Upper Great Lakes with a water level less than 465 feet above present sea level but higher than the Chippewa-Stanley stage level.

LAKE AGASSIZ. An extinct glacial lake named for Louis Agassiz. It covered large parts of Minnesota, North Dakota, Manitoba, and western Ontario. It was in existence from some time prior to 10,000 B.C. and lasted until after about 4000 B.C.

LAKE ALGONQUIN. A glacial lake stage in the basins of Lake Huron and Lake Michigan. It had a water level of 605 feet above the present sea level.

LAKE CHICAGO. A glacial lake in the southern half of the Lake Michigan basin. Its stages are Glenwood at 640 feet and Calumet at 620 feet above present sea level.

LAKE CHIPPEWA. A postglacial lake in the Lake Michigan basin during the Chippewa-Stanley stage. It stood at 230 feet above present sea level.

LAKE NIPISSING. A lake northeast of Georgian Bay in Ontario, Canada.

LAKE NIPISSING STAGE. A postglacial stage of the Upper Great Lakes with a water level at 605 feet above present sea level.

LAKE OJIBWA-BARLOW. An extinct glacial lake in northern Ontario formerly lying between the height of land and the Hudson's Bay ice lobe.

LAKE STANLEY. A postglacial lake in the Lake Huron basin during the Chippewa-Stanley stage. It stood at 180 feet or less above present sea level.

LALONDE CULTURE. An Indian culture of the Late Woodland period in Ontario.

LANCEOLATE POINTS. A point of stone, bone, or metal shaped somewhat like a willow leaf.

LATE VALDERS RETREAT. A period late in the retreat of the Valders glacier about 7000 to 6000 B.C.

LATE WOODLAND INDIANS. Indians representative of the various cultures of the Late Woodland period about A.D. 800 to 1600.

LATER LAKE OSHKOSH. An extinct glacial lake that occupied the basin of present-day Lake Winnebago in Wisconsin.

LATER POSTGLACIAL. A period after the disappearance of the glacial ice. It lasted from about 1500 to 500 B.C.

LOWER GREAT LAKES REGION. The region bordering Lake Erie and Lake Ontario.

MAMMOTH. An extinct kind of elephant. Mammoths were grazing animals and lived in grasslands.

MANITO. Word for spirit or supernatural power in a number of different languages of the Algonkian family of languages.

MASTODON. An extinct kind of elephant. Mastodons were browsing animals and lived in forested regions. They ate leaves, twigs, and more tender parts of trees and shrubs, as well as grasses.

MATRILINEAL. The reckoning of descent in the female line.

MENOMINI. A tribe of Indians living on the northwestern border of Lake Michigan at the time of the first arrival of Europeans.

MIAMI. An Indian tribe living in the southern Lake Michigan area at the time of the first arrival of Europeans.

MICHIGAN OWASCO CULTURE. A culture of the Late Woodland period in eastern Michigan and adjacent parts of Ontario.

MIDDLE VALDERS RETREAT. A period while Valders glacier was retreating northward but was still present in the eastern part of the Lake Superior basin. The period was from about 8000 to 7000 B.C.

MIDDLE WOODLAND PERIOD. The period of the Middle Woodland cultures in the Upper Great Lakes region lasting from about 100 B.C. to A.D. 700 or 800.

MIDEWIWIN. The name for a religious organization, the Grand Medicine Society, in any one of several Algonkian languages.

MINONG STAGE. A lake stage in the Lake Superior basin later than the Algonquin stage in the Huron and Michigan basins.

MORAINE. An accumulation of earth, stones, clay, and sand carried and deposited by a glacier.

MOUND-BUILDERS. Any group of American Indians that erected mounds. Any other use of this term in American archeology is incorrect.

NASSAUKETON. A band or large division of the Ottawa tribe of Indians.

NIPISSING STAGE. A postglacial stage of the Upper Great Lakes with a water level at 605 feet above present sea level.

NORTH BAY OUTLET. An abandoned channel from North Bay, Ontario (northeast of Georgian Bay), down the Mattawa Valley to the Ottawa River. In past times it was an outlet of the Upper Great Lakes.

OBSIDIAN. Volcanic glass, a dark-colored glassy stone that can be flaked and chipped like flint.

OJIBWA. Another name for the Chippewa tribe of Indians.

OLD COPPER CULTURE. A particular variety of Boreal Archaic culture marked by specialization in the manufacture of copper artifacts.

OSSUARIES. Mass burials in a common grave.

OTTAWA INDIANS. A tribe of Indians living in the northeastern part of the Upper Great Lakes region at the time of the first arrival of Europeans.

PALEOGEOGRAPHY. The study and interpretation of surface features of the earth that existed in past times and do not exist today.

PALEO-INDIANS. Indians who lived in America in glacial times.

PALYNOLOGIST. A scientist specializing in the study of fossil pollens and their associations and relationships.

PAN-INDIAN CULTURE. A culture common to a number of different tribes of Indians at a given time, in a given place. As used in this work it indicates a number of different cultures tending to become one common culture.

PANPIPE. A musical instrument consisting of a number of conjoined tubes or pipes of different lengths. When the player blows across or into the tubes different tones are produced.

PARALLEL-FLAKING. The act of removing flakes so that the flake scars are more or less parallel. Such technique produces the appearance of parallel ridges and valleys on a stone weapon point or blade.

PATRILINEAL. The reckoning of descent in the male line.

PAYETTE STAGE. A post-Algonquin stage in the Upper Great Lakes with a water level at about 465 feet above present sea level.

PENETANG STAGE. A post-Algonquin stage in the Upper Great Lakes with a water level at about 510 feet above present sea level.

PENINSULAR WOODLAND CULTURE. The culture of Indians who lived in parts of the Lake Michigan basin and the Lake Superior basin in the Late Woodland period.

PEOPLE OF THE FORK. A large band or division of the Ottawa tribe of Indians.

PHRATRY. A group of clans within a tribe.

PLANO POINTS. A number of different varieties of leaf-shaped points associated with ancient Indian cultures in the West and sometimes also with extinct animals, particularly members of the bison family.

PLEISTOCENE. The Ice Age—a division of time used by geologists.

POLYGAMY. Plural marriage, such as a woman with more than one husband or a man with more than one wife.

POLYGYNY. The form of polygamy in which a man has more than one wife.

PORT HURON GLACIAL ADVANCE. The advance of the glacier that deposited the Port Huron moraine in the period of 11,000 to 10,000 B.C.

PORT HURON OUTLET. A former channel through which the Upper Great Lakes drained during certain past stages. It was situated near Port Huron, Michigan, where at the present time there is a similar but lower outlet of the Upper Lakes.

POSTGLACIAL PERIOD. The period following the disappearance of the glacier from all parts of the region. This period is from about 3000 B.C. to the present time.

POTAWATOMI. A tribe of Indians living in the northern Lake Michigan area at the time of first arrival of Europeans.

POTSHERD. Any broken piece of pottery or earthenware.

PREHISTORY. What happened in a given region before the time of recorded history in that region.

PROTOHISTORIC. Immediately preceding the time of the beginning of written history in a region.

QUADRILOBATE. Having four lobes or bulges.

QUARTZITE. A rock composed essentially of the mineral quartz. The different quartzites used by the Indians could be flaked and chipped like flint. Quartzite is a metamorphosed sandstone.

RED OCHER. A red earthy, often impure, variety of the sesquioxide of iron (Fe_2O_0) used as a pigment.

RIPPLE-FLAKING. A kind of parallel-flaking of flint that produces a surface that looks as if it had ripples.

SAUK INDIANS. A tribe of Indians living in the southwestern part of the Upper Great Lakes region at the time of the first arrival of Europeans.

SHAMAN. A medicine man who performed healing of the sick by a combination of natural means and supposed magico-religious powers.

SHEGUIANDAH STAGE. A post-Algonquin lake stage in the Upper Great Lakes region. Its water level was somewhere between 390 and 465 feet above present sea level.

SHELL-TEMPERING. The addition of small pieces of crushed shell to clay before making pottery. Shell-tempering material was supposed to prevent the pottery from cracking when fired to harden it.

SHERD. Any broken piece of pottery or earthenware.

SINAGO. A band or large division of the Ottawa tribe of Indians.

SLATE. A kind of rock, a metamorphosed mud stone or shale.

SPEAR-THROWER. An implement that makes it possible to hurl a spear farther and with greater force than with the arm only. The butt of the spear is engaged by the outer end of the spear-thrower which functions as a mechanical extension of the arm.

STRATIGRAPHY. The method of determining relative age or order in a sequence of events by means of superposition. In ordinary stratification by layers, the oldest is on the bottom and the youngest at the top.

TACONITE. A rock that will flake or chip somewhat like flint. It is a low-grade iron ore found in the Lake Superior region.

TERMINAL GLACIAL PERIOD. The period in which the glacier disappeared from the northernmost part of the extended Upper Great Lakes region. This period was from about 6000 to 3000 B.C.

TIONONTATI INDIANS. Another name for the Tobacco Huron Indians.

TOBACCO HURON. A tribe of Indians closely related by language, custom, and mode of life to the Huron Indians, their neighbors in the southern Georgian Bay area of Ontario.

TOLESTON STAGE. A former lake stage in the Lake Michigan basin. It is related in time and elevation to the early part of the Lake Algonquin stage.

TRAIT, CULTURAL. Any single element or any individual part of human behavior that expresses culture. For example, pottery-making, mound-building, and use of copper for tools are cultural traits.

TRIBE. A large group of people bound together by the ties of language, kinship, and custom. A tribe as used in this book is similar to a nation.

"TURKEY TAIL" BLADE OR POINT. A spear point or blade of chipped flint with a base that in silhouette resembles the posterior of a plucked turkey as viewed by the person carving this fowl at a dinner.

TWO CREEKS INTERSTADIAL. A period of glacial retreat lasting from about 10,000 to 9000 B.C.

UPPER GREAT LAKES REGION. The region containing the drainage basins of Lake Superior, Lake Michigan, and Lake Huron.

VALDERS ADVANCE. The advance of the Valders glacier between 9000 and 8500 B.C. in the Upper Great Lakes region.

VALDERS RED TILL. Unstratified glacial material deposited directly by the ice and consisting of red clay, sand, gravel, and boulders in varying proportions.

VARVE. One of a series of seasonally banded layers of clay or fine silt deposited in glacial lakes.

WESTERN GREAT LAKES REGION. Another name for Upper Great Lakes region.

WINNEBAGO. A tribe of Indians that occupied the area by Lake Winnebago in Wisconsin.

WYEBRIDGE STAGE. A post-Algonquin lake stage in the Upper Great Lakes region. Its water level was 540 feet above present sea level.

ANTEVS, ERNST
1928   *The Last Glaciation.* ("American Geographical Society, Research Series," No. 17.) New York.

BAERREIS, D. A., DAIFUKU, HIROSHI, and LUNSTED, J. E.
1954   "The Burial Complex of the Reigh Site, Winnebago County, Wisconsin," *Wisconsin Archeologist,* **35,** No. 1, 1–36. Milwaukee.

BLAIR, EMMA HELEN
1911   *The Indian Tribes of the Upper Mississippi Valley and Region of the Great Lakes as Described by Nicolas Perrot, French Commandant in the Northwest; Bacquevelle de la Potherie, French Royal Commissioner to Canada; Morrell Marston, American Army Officer; and Thomas Forsyth, United States Agent at Fort Armstrong.* 2 vols. Cleveland.

BLUHM, ELAINE, and WENNER, DAVID J., JR.
1956   "Prehistoric Culture of Chicago Area Uncovered," *Chicago Natural History Museum Bulletin,* **27,** No. 2, 5–6. Chicago.

BRETZ, J HARLEN
1951   "The Stages of Lake Chicago: Their Causes and Correlations," *American Journal of Science,* **249,** No. 6, 401–29. New Haven.

BROECKER, W. S., and KULP, J. L.
1955   "Lamont C14 Studies," *Bulletin of the Geological Society of America,* **66,** No. 12, Part 2, 1535–36. New York.
1956   "The Radiocarbon Method of Age Determination," *American Antiquity,* **22,** No. 1, 1–11. Salt Lake City.

BYERS, DOUGLAS S.
1959   "The Eastern Archaic: Some Problems and Hypotheses," *American Antiquity,* **24,** No. 3, 233–56. Salt Lake City.

CRANE, H. R.
1956   "University of Michigan Radiocarbon Dates I," *Science,* **124,** No. 3224, 664–72. Washington, D.C.

CRANE, H. R., and GRIFFIN, JAMES B.
1958   "University of Michigan Radiocarbon Dates II," *Science,* **127,** No. 3306, 1098–1105. Washington, D.C.

CUNNINGHAM, WILBUR M.
1948 A Study of the Glacial Kame Culture in Michigan, Ohio, and Indiana. ("Occasional Contributions from the Museum of Anthropology of the University of Michigan," No. 12.) Ann Arbor.

DEEVEY, EDWARD S., and FLINT, RICHARD FOSTER
1957 "Postglacial Hypsithermal Interval," Science, **125,** No. 3240, 182–84. Washington, D.C.

DEUEL, THORNE
1952 "Hopewellian Dress in Illinois," in Archeology of Eastern United States, ed. JAMES B. GRIFFIN, pp. 165–75. Chicago.

DORSEY, J. OWEN, and RADIN, PAUL
1912 "Winnebago," in Handbook of American Indians North of Mexico, ed. F. W. HODGE, pp. 958–61. (Bureau of American Ethnology Bulletin No. 30, Part II.) Washington, D.C.

ELSON, JOHN A.
1957 "Lake Agassiz and the Mankato-Valders Problem," Science, **126,** No. 3281, 999–1002. Washington, D.C.

ERICSON, D. B., BROECKER, W. S., KULP, J. L., and WOLLIN, GOESTA
1956 "Late-Pleistocene Climates and Deep-Sea Sediments," Science, **124,** No. 3218, 385–89. Washington, D.C.

FENTON, WILLIAM N.
1940 "Problems Arising from the Historic Northeastern Position of the Iroquois," in Essays in Historical Anthropology of North America. ("Smithsonian Miscellaneous Collections," **100,** 159–251.) Washington, D.C.

FOX, GEORGE R.
1930 "A MacGregor Bay Cemetery," Wisconsin Archeologist, **10,** No. 2, 61–64. Milwaukee.

GIBSON, EDMOND P.
1954 "Ancient Mounds near Grand Rapids in the Lower Grand River Valley and in Southwestern Michigan," Michigan Archaeological Society News, **1,** No. 3, 3–10. Ann Arbor.

GJESSING, GUTORM
1948 "Some Problems in Northeastern Archaeology," American Antiquity, **13,** No. 4, 298–302. Menasha, Wis.

GOODE, J. PAUL
1937 Goode's School Atlas. New York.

GREEN, AMOS

1954 "An Earthwork Inclosure near Sumnerville," *Michigan Archaeological Society News,* **1,** No. 4, 1–3. Ann Arbor.

GREENMAN, EMERSON F.

1927 "Michigan Mounds with Special Reference to Two in Missaukee County," *Papers of the Michigan Academy of Science, Arts, and Letters,* **7,** pp. 1–9. Ann Arbor.

1937 *The Younge Site: An Archaeological Record from Michigan.* ("Occasional Contributions from the Museum of Anthropology of the University of Michigan," No. 6.) Ann Arbor.

1939 *The Wolf and Furton Sites, Macomb County, Michigan.* ("Occasional Contributions from the Museum of Anthropology of the University of Michigan," No. 8.) Ann Arbor.

1943 "An Early Industry on a Raised Beach near Killarney, Ontario," *American Antiquity,* **8,** No. 3, 260–95. Menasha, Wis.

1948 "The Killarney Sequence and Its Old World Connections," *Papers of the Michigan Academy of Science, Arts, and Letters,* **32,** 313–32. Ann Arbor.

1951 *Old Birch Island Cemetery and the Early Historic Trade Route, Georgian Bay, Ontario.* ("Occasional Contributions from the Museum of Anthropology of the University of Michigan," No. 11.) Ann Arbor.

1953 "Review of 'Sixty Years of Ontario Archeology' by Kenneth E. Kidd and 'The Archeology of the Upper Great Lakes Area' by George I. Quimby," *American Antiquity,* **19,** No. 2, 176–77. Salt Lake City.

1955 "Wave Action at George Lake I, Ontario," *American Antiquity,* **20,** No. 4, 376–77. Salt Lake City.

GREENMAN, EMERSON F., and STANLEY, GEORGE M.

1940 "A Geologically Dated Camp Site, Georgian Bay, Ontario," *American Antiquity,* **5,** No. 3, 194–99. Menasha, Wis.

1941 "Two Post-Nipissing Sites near Killarney, Ontario," *American Antiquity,* **6,** No. 4, 305–13. Menasha, Wis.

1943 "The Archaeology and Geology of Two Early Sites near Killarney, Ontario," *Papers of the Michigan Academy of Science, Arts, and Letters,* **28,** 505–31. Ann Arbor.

GRIFFIN, JAMES B.

1943 *The Fort Ancient Aspect: Its Cultural and Chronological Position in Mississippi Valley Archaeology.* Ann Arbor.

1956 "The Reliability of Radiocarbon Dates for Late Glacial and Recent Times in Central and Eastern North America," *University of Utah Anthropological Papers*, No. 26, pp. 10–34. Salt Lake City.

1958 Personal communication.

GUTHE, CARL E.

n.d. Field notes.

HANDLEY, CHARLES O., JR.

1953 "Marine Mammals in Michigan," *Journal of Mammology*, **34**, No. 2, 252–53. Baltimore.

HATT, ROBERT T., et al.

1948 *Island Life: A Study of the Land Vertebrates of the Islands of Eastern Lake Michigan.* (Cranbrook Institute of Science Bulletin No. 27.) Bloomfield Hills, Mich.

HEARNE, SAMUEL

1795 *A Journey from Prince of Wale's Fort in Hudson's Bay, to the Northern Ocean.* London.

HENRY, ALEXANDER

1809 *Travels and Adventures in Canada and the Indian Territories between the Years 1760 and 1776*, ed. JAMES BAIN, 1901. Toronto.

HEWITT, J. N. B.

1912 "Sauk," in *Handbook of American Indians North of Mexico*, ed. F. W. HODGE, pp. 471–80. (Bureau of American Ethnology Bulletin No. 30, Part II.) Washington, D.C.

HINSDALE, WILBERT B.

1929 "Indian Mounds, West Twin Lake, Montmorency County, Michigan," *Papers of the Michigan Academy of Science, Arts, and Letters*, **10**, 91–101. Ann Arbor.

1930 "Reports of Archaeological Field Work in the Summer of 1928 in Montmorency, Newaygo, and Lake Counties, Michigan," *Papers of the Michigan Academy of Science, Arts, and Letters*, **11**, 127–35. Ann Arbor.

1932 *Distribution of the Aboriginal Population of Michigan.* ("Occasional Contributions from the Museum of Anthropology of the University of Michigan," No. 2.) Ann Arbor.

HOFFMAN, WALTER J.

1893 "The Menomini Indians." *14th Annual Report, Bureau of American Ethnology.* Washington, D.C.

Hoijer, Harry, et al.
  1946 Linguistic Structures of Native America. ("Viking Fund Publications in Anthropology," No. 6.) New York.

Hough, Jack L.
  1953 Pleistocene Chronology of the Great Lakes Region. (Final Report on Project NR-018-122, Office of Naval Research.) Urbana: University of Illinois. (Mimeographed.)
  1958 Geology of the Great Lakes. Urbana.

Jenks, Albert E.
  1937 Minnesota's Browns Valley Man and Associated Burial Artifacts. ("Memoirs of the American Anthropological Association," No. 49.) Menasha, Wis.

Jury, Wilfred, and Jury, Elsie
  1952 "The Burley Site," University of Western Ontario Museum of Archaeology and Pioneer Life Bulletin, No. 9, pp. 57–75. London, Ontario.

Keesing, Felix M.
  1939 The Menomini Indians of Wisconsin. ("Memoirs of the American Philosophical Society," Vol. **10.**) Philadelphia.

Kidd, Kenneth E.
  1952 "Sixty Years of Ontario Archeology," in Archeology of the Eastern United States, ed. J. B. Griffin, pp. 71–82. Chicago.
  1954 "A Woodland Site Near Chatham, Ontario," Transactions of the Royal Canadian Institute, **30,** Part 2, pp. 141–78. Toronto.

Kinietz, W. Vernon
  1940 The Indians of the Western Great Lakes 1615–1760. ("Occasional Contributions from the Museum of Anthropology of the University of Michigan," No. 10.) Ann Arbor.

Kroeber, A. L.
  1939 Cultural and Natural Areas of Native North America. ("University of California Publications in American Archaeology and Ethnology," Vol. **38.**) Berkeley.

Lawson, Publius V.
  1907 "The Winnebago Tribe," Wisconsin Archeologist, **6,** No. 3, 77–162. Madison.

Lee, Thomas E.
  1951 "A Preliminary Report on an Archaeological Survey of Southwestern Ontario in 1949," Bulletin of the National Museum of Canada, No. 123, pp. 42–48. Ottawa.

1952 "A Preliminary Report of an Archaeological Survey of Southwestern Ontario for 1950," *Bulletin of the National Museum of Canada*, No. 126, pp. 64–75. Ottawa.

1953 "A Preliminary Report on the Sheguiandah Site, Manitoulin Island," *Bulletin of the National Museum of Canada*, No. 128, pp. 58–67. Ottawa.

1954 "The First Sheguiandah Expedition, Manitoulin Island, Ontario," *American Antiquity*, **20**, 101–11. Salt Lake City.

1955 "The Second Sheguiandah Expedition, Manitoulin Island, Ontario," *American Antiquity*, **21**, 63–71. Salt Lake City.

1956 "The Position and Meaning of a Radiocarbon Sample from the Sheguiandah Site, Ontario," *American Antiquity*, **22**, No. 1, 79. Salt Lake City.

1957 "The Antiquity of the Sheguiandah Site," *Canadian Field Naturalist*, **71**, No. 3, 117–37. Ottawa.

1958 "The Parker Earthwork, Corunna, Ontario," *Pennsylvania Archaeologist*, **28**, No. 1, 3–29. Honesdale, Pa.

LIBBY, WILLARD F.

1952 *Radiocarbon Dating*. Chicago.

LISS, ALLEN, and BLUHM, ELAINE.

1958 "Museum Aids in Chicago Area Salvage Dig," *Chicago Natural History Museum Bulletin*, **29**, No. 11, 6. Chicago.

LONG, JOHN

1791 *Voyages and Travels of an Indian Interpreter and Trader etc.* London.

MacALPIN, ARCHIE

1940 "A Census of Mastodon Remains in Michigan," *Papers of the Michigan Academy of Science, Arts, and Letters*, **25**, 481–90. Ann Arbor.

McKERN, WILL C.

1928 *The Neale and McClaughry Mound Groups*. (Milwaukee Public Museum Bulletin, Vol. **3**, No. 3.) Milwaukee.

1930 *The Kletzien and Nitschke Mound Groups*. (Milwaukee Public Museum Bulletin, Vol. **3**, No. 4.) Milwaukee.

1942 "First Settlers of Wisconsin," *Wisconsin Magazine of History*, **26**, No. 2, 153–69. Madison.

1945 *Preliminary Report on the Upper Mississippi Phase in Wisconsin*. (Milwaukee Public Museum Bulletin, Vol. **16**, No. 2.) Milwaukee.

MacNEISH, RICHARD S.

1952 "A Possible Early Site in the Thunder Bay District, Ontario," *Bulletin of the National Museum of Canada 1950–51*, No. 126, pp. 23–47. Ottawa.

MARIE-VICTORIN, FRERE

1938 "Phyto-geographical Problems of Eastern Canada," *The American Midland Naturalist*, **19,** No. 3, 489–558. Notre Dame, Ind.

MASON, RONALD J.

1958 *Late Pleistocene Geochronology and the Paleo-Indian Penetration into the Lower Michigan Peninsula.* ("Anthropological Papers," No. 11.) Ann Arbor: Museum of Anthropology, University of Michigan.

1959 Personal communication.

MELHORN, W. N.

1956 "Valders Drift in the Southern Peninsula of Michigan," in *Guidebook*, pp. 13–19. Ann Arbor: Friends of the Pleistocene, Midwest Section.

MEYER, ALFRED H.

1952 "Fundament Vegetation of the Calumet Region, Northwest Indiana— Northeast Illinois," *Papers of the Michigan Academy of Science, Arts, and Letters,* **36,** 177–82. Ann Arbor.

MICHELSON, TRUMAN

1911 "Note on the Gentes of the Ottawa," *American Anthropologist,* **13,** 338. Lancaster, Pa.

MOONEY, JAMES, and HEWITT, J. N. B.

1912a "Ottawa," in *Handbook of American Indians North of Mexico*, ed. F. W. HODGE, pp. 167–71. (Bureau of American Ethnology Bulletin No. 30, Part II.) Washington, D.C.

1912b "Potawatomi," in *Handbook of American Indians North of Mexico*, ed. F. W. HODGE, pp. 289–91. (Bureau of American Ethnology Bulletin No. 30, Part II.) Washington, D.C.

MOONEY, JAMES, and THOMAS, CYRUS

1912a "Chippewa," in *Handbook of American Indians North of Mexico*, ed. F. W. HODGE, pp. 277–80. (Bureau of American Ethnology Bulletin No. 30, Part I.) Washington, D.C.

1912b "Foxes," in *Handbook of American Indians North of Mexico*, ed. F. W. HODGE, pp. 472–74. (Bureau of American Ethnology Bulletin No. 30, Part I.) Washington, D.C.

1912c "Menominee," in *Handbook of American Indians North of Mexico*, ed. F. W. HODGE, pp. 842–43. (Bureau of American Ethnology Bulletin No. 30, Part I.) Washington, D.C.

POPHAM, ROBERT E.

1950 "Late Huron Occupations of Ontario: An Archaeological Survey of Innisfil Township," *Ontario History,* **42,** No. 2, 81–90. Toronto.

POPHAM, R. E., and EMERSON, J. N.

1954 "Manifestations of the Old Copper Industry in Ontario," *Pennsylvania Archaeologist*, **24,** No. 1, 3–19. Honesdale, Pa.

PRESTON, R. S., PERSON, E., and DEEVEY, E. S.

1955 "Yale Natural Radiocarbon Measurements II," *Science*, **22,** No. 3177, 954–60. Washington, D.C.

QUIMBY, GEORGE I.

n.d. Field notes.

1937 "Notes on Indian Trade Silver Ornaments in Michigan," *Papers of the Michigan Academy of Science, Arts, and Letters*, **22,** 15–24. Ann Arbor.

1938 "Dated Indian Burials in Michigan," *Papers of the Michigan Academy of Science, Arts, and Letters*, **23,** 63–75. Ann Arbor.

1939 "European Trade Articles as Chronological Indicators for the Archaeology of the Historic Period in Michigan," *Papers of the Michigan Academy of Science, Arts, and Letters*, **24,** 25–31. Ann Arbor.

1940 "Some Notes on Kinship and Kinship Terminology among the Potawatomi of the Huron," *Papers of the Michigan Academy of Science, Arts, and Letters*, **25,** 553–63. Ann Arbor.

1941a *The Goodall Focus: An Analysis of Ten Hopewellian Components in Michigan and Indiana.* ("Indiana Historical Society Prehistory Research Series," **2,** No. 2, 63–161.) *Indianapolis.*

1941b "Hopewellian Pottery Types in Michigan," *Papers of the Michigan Academy of Science, Arts, and Letters*, **26,** 489–95. Ann Arbor.

1943a "The Ceramic Sequence within the Goodall Focus," *Papers of the Michigan Academy of Science, Arts, and Letters*, **28,** 543–48. Ann Arbor.

1943b "A Subjective Interpretation of Some Design Similarities between Hopewell and Northern Algonkian," *American Anthropologist*, **45,** No. 4, 630–33. Menasha, Wis.

1944 "Some New Data on the Goodall Focus," *Papers of the Michigan Academy of Science, Arts, and Letters*, **29,** 419–23. Ann Arbor.

1949 "A Hopewell Tool for Decorating Pottery," *American Antiquity*, **14,** No. 4, 344. Menasha, Wis.

1954 "The Old Copper Assemblage and Extinct Animals," *American Antiquity*, **20,** No. 2, 169–70. Salt Lake City.

1957 "An Old Copper Site at Menominee, Michigan," *Wisconsin Archeologist*, **38,** No. 2, 37–41. Milwaukee.

1958a "Fluted Points and Geochronology of the Lake Michigan Basin," *American Antiquity*, **23,** No. 3, 247–54. Salt Lake City.

1958b "Late Archaic Culture and the Algoma Beach in the Lake Michigan Basin," *Wisconsin Archeologist*, **39**, No. 3, 175–79. Milwaukee.

1958c "New Evidence Links Chippewa to Prehistoric Culture," *Chicago Natural History Museum Bulletin*, **29**, No. 1, 7–8. Chicago.

1958d "Silver Ornaments and the Indians," *Miscellanea Paul Rivet Octogenario Dicata, XXXI Congreso Internacional de Americanistas*, Part I, pp. 317–37. Mexico, D.F.: Universidad Nacional Autonoma de Mexico.

QUIMBY, GEORGE I., and SPAULDING, ALBERT C.
1957   *The Old Copper Culture and the Keweenaw Waterway* ("Fieldiana Anthropology," **36**, No. 8, 189–201.) Chicago.

RADIN, PAUL
1923   "The Winnebago Tribe," *37th Annual Report, Bureau of American Ethnology*. Washington, D.C.

RIDLEY, FRANK
1952a   "Huron and Lalonde Occupations of Ontario," *American Antiquity*, **17**, No. 3, 197–210. Salt Lake City.

1952b   "The Fallis Site, Ontario," *American Antiquity*, **18**, No. 1, 7–14. Salt Lake City.

1954   "The Frank Bay Site, Lake Nipissing, Ontario," *American Antiquity*, **20**, No. 1, 40–50. Salt Lake City.

1958   *The Boys and Barrie Sites.* ("Publication No. 4 of the Ontario Archaeological Society.") Toronto.

RITZENTHALER, ROBERT E.
1953   *The Potawatomi Indians of Wisconsin* (Milwaukee Public Museum Bulletin, Vol. **19**, No. 3.) Milwaukee.

1958   "Some Carbon 14 Dates for the Wisconsin Old Copper Culture," *Wisconsin Archaeologist*, **39**, No. 3, 173–74. Milwaukee.

RITZENTHALER, ROBERT, et al.
1956   "Reigh Site Report—Number 3," *Wisconsin Archeologist*, **37**, No. 4, 97–129. Milwaukee.

RITZENTHALER, ROBERT, and WITTRY, WARREN L.
1952   "The Oconto Site—an Old Copper Manifestation," *Wisconsin Archeologist*, **33**, No. 4, pp. 199–223. Milwaukee.

ROWE, CHANDLER W.
1956   *The Effigy Mound Culture of Wisconsin.* ("Milwaukee Public Museum Publications in Anthropology," No. 3.) Milwaukee.

SHARP, R. P.
   1953   "Shorelines of the Glacial Great Lakes in Cook County, Minnesota,"
         American Journal of Science, **251** (February), 109–39. New Haven.

SPAULDING, ALBERT C.
   1946   "Northeastern Archaeology and General Trends in the Northern Forest
         Zone," in *Man in Northeastern North America,* ed. FREDERICK JOHNSON,
         pp. 143–67. Andover, Mass.
   1957   "Old Copper Culture," in "Arctic Notes and News," *American Antiquity,*
         22, No. 4, 436–37. Salt Lake City.
   1957a "Eskimo at the Reigh Site?" *Wisconsin Archeologist,* **38,** No. 1, 30–31.
         Milwaukee.
   1958   "The Significance of Differences between Radiocarbon Dates," *American
         Antiquity,* **23,** No. 3, 309–11. Salt Lake City.

SPURR, S. H., and ZUMBERGE, J. H.
   1956   "Late Pleistocene Features of Cheboygan and Emmet Counties, Michi-
         gan," *American Journal of Science,* **254** (February), 96–109. New Haven.

STANLEY, GEORGE M.
   1937   "Lower Algonquin Beaches of Cape Rich, Georgian Bay," *Bulletin of the
         Geological Society of America,* **48,** 1665–86. New York.
   1938   "The Submerged Valley through Mackinac Straits," *Journal of Geology,*
         46, 966–74. Chicago.
   1941   "Minong Beaches and Water Planes in Lake Superior Basin," *Bulletin of
         the Geological Society of America,* **52,** 1935. New York.
   1943   *See* GREENMAN and STANLEY, 1943.
   1948   *See* HATT, 1948, pp. 11–22.
   1953   *See* SHARP, 1953, p. 128.

SWANTON, J. R.
   1952   *The Indian Tribes of North America.* (Bureau of American Ethnology
         Bulletin No. 145.) Washington, D.C.

TAX, SOL
   1937   "The Social Organization of the Fox Indians," in *Social Anthropology of
         North American Indians,* ed. FRED EGGAN, pp. 241–82. Chicago.

THWAITES, F. T.
   1943   "Pleistocene of Part of Northeastern Wisconsin," *Bulletin of the Geo-
         logical Society of America,* **54,** No. 1, 87–144. New York.

THWAITES, F. T., and BERTRAND, KENNETH
   1957   "Pleistocene Geology of the Door Peninsula, Wisconsin," *Bulletin of the
         Geological Society of America,* **68,** No. 7, 831–80. New York.

WINTEMBERG, W. J.
   1946   "The Sidey-Mackay Village Site," *American Antiquity,* **11,** No. 3, 154–82. Menasha, Wis.

WITTRY, WARREN L.
   1951   "A Preliminary Study of the Old Copper Complex," *Wisconsin Archeologist,* **32,** No. 1, 1–18. Milwaukee.

WITTRY, W. L., and RITZENTHALER, R. E.
   1956   "The Old Copper Complex: An Archaic Manifestation in Wisconsin," *American Antiquity,* **21,** No. 3, 244–54. Salt Lake City.

WORMINGTON, H. M.
   1957   *Ancient Man in North America.* ("Denver Museum of Natural History Popular Series," No. 4.) Denver.

WRAY, DONALD E.
   1952   "Archeology of the Illinois Valley: 1950," in *Archeology of Eastern United States,* ed. JAMES B. GRIFFIN, pp. 152–64. Chicago.

ZIM, H. S., and HOFFMEISTER, D. F.
   1955   *Mammals: A Guide to Familiar American Species.* New York.

ZUMBERGE, J. H.
   1956   "Late Pleistocene History of the Lake Michigan Basin," in *Guidebook,* pp. 3–12. Ann Arbor: Friends of the Pleistocene, Midwest Section.

ZUMBERGE, J. H., and POTZGER, J. E.
   1956   "Late Wisconsin Chronology of the Lake Michigan Basin Correlated with Pollen Studies," *Bulletin of the Geological Society of America,* **67,** No. 3, 271–88. New York.

INDEX

Acculturation, 111, 112, 154

Adzes, first appearance in region, 43, 44. *See also* Tools

Agassiz. *See* Lake Agassiz

Agate Basin points, 35

Agriculture: Blue Island, 105; Chippewa, 123; Effigy Mound, 87; Fisher, 100; Fox, 133; Hopewell, 73; Huron, 114; introduction into region, 80, 81; Lake Winnebago, 103; Lalonde, 98; Menomini, 143; Miami, 133; Michigan Owasco, 94; Ottawa, 128; Pan-Indian, 148; Peninsular Woodland, 88; Potawatomi, 128; Sauk, 133; Winnebago, 140

Algoma stage, 17, 26, 159

Algonkian language, 110

Algonquin stage. *See* Lake Algonquin stage

Angostura points, 34

Animals hunted: Boreal Archaic, 44; Chippewa, 122; Early Woodland, 66; Fisher, 101, Fox, 134; Lake Winnebago, 103; Lalonde, 98; Miami, 134; Michigan Owasco, 94; Old Copper, 56; Ottawa, 128; Potawatomi, 128; Sauk, 134

Animals introduced by French, 112

Antevs, Ernst, 16

Aqua-Plano culture, 34–42, 159; artifacts from Brohm site, 36, 37; artifacts from Browns Valley site, 35; artifacts from George Lake site, 39; artifacts from Sheguiandah site, 39; burial, 34, 35, 41; climate, 40; environment, 40, 41; fauna, 41; flora, 41; geology of sites, 34, 35, 36, 37, 38, 39, 40; livelihood, 41; summary of culture, 41; tools, 35, 36, 37, 39; weapons, 35, 36, 37, 39

Aqua-Plano period, 6, 34–42

Argillite, 42, 44, 47, 159

Armor, 117

Arrows and arrowheads. *See* Weapons

Art, 79, 80

Axes, first appearance of, 43, 44. *See also* Tools

Bands: Chippewa, 122; Huron, 118, 119; Ottawa, 128, 129; Potawatomi, 128, 129

Bannerstones, 45, 159

Bar amulets, 49

Barren-ground caribou, 20, 21, 22, 24, 25, 56, 61

Beads. *See* Ornaments

Birdstones, 49, 68

Blue Island culture, 105–6, 159; agriculture, 105; burial, 106; dwellings, 105; environment, 105; livelihood, 105; ornaments, 106; pipes, 106; pottery, 105, 106; tools, 106; weapons, 106

Boats, 3, 41, 56, 58, 124, 129, 134, 142, 143

Boreal Archaic culture, 6, 7, 43–51, 159; animals hunted, 44; adzes, 43, 44; axes, 43, 44; burial, 49; climax of, 49; dwellings, 45; fauna, 44; fishing, 45; flora, 43, 44; gouges, 43, 44; hunting, 44; livelihood, 44; ornaments, 49; red ocher, 35, 49; relation to Old Copper culture, 43, 50, 51; spear-thrower, 44, 45; tools, 43, 44, 47; utensils 47; weapons, 44, 45, 49; woodworking tools, 43, 44

Bowmanville stage. *See* Two Creeks low-water stage

Bows and arrows. *See* Weapons

Bretz, J. H., 11, 14

Brohm site, 36, 37, 38, 159

Browns Valley site, 34, 35

Burial: Aqua-Plano, 34, 35, 41; Blue Island, 106; Boreal Archaic, 49; Early Woodland, 64, 70; Effigy Mound, 85, 87; Fisher, 102; Fox, 139; Hopewell, 80; Huron, 120; 121; Lake Winnebago, 105; Miami, 139; Michigan Owasco, 97, 98; Middle Woodland, 83; Old Copper, 58; Ottawa, 132; Pan-Indian, 154, 156, 157; Peninsular Woodland, 91, 92; Potawatomi, 132; Sauk, 139; Winnebago, 142

Calendar, Menomini, 144

Calumet stage, 14, 17, 28, 30, 159

Canoe. *See* Boats

Cedar Point stage, 15, 22, 40, 159

Celt. *See* Tools

Ceremonial centers of Hopewell, 72, 73, 74

Ceremonial life in Early Woodland culture, 70

Ceremonial structures of Michigan Owasco, 94, 95

Chicago outlet, 14, 16, 22, 25

Chinese porcelain, 148, 157

Chippewa, 7, 93, 122–27, 159

Chippewa culture, 122–27; agriculture, 123; animals hunted, 122; bands, 122; clans, 126; dwellings, 124; environment, 122; fauna, 122; Feast of the Dead, 126; fishing, 122,